The World Needs *Old Ladies*

They Are the Tree of Life

By

*Gladys T. McGarey M.D., M.D. (H)
and Eveline Horelle Dailey*

The World Needs *Old Ladies*

They Are the Tree of Life

By

*Gladys T. McGarey M.D., M.D. (H)
and Eveline Horelle Dailey*

A Collaboration

▲INKWELL PRODUCTIONS®

Copyright 2013
By Gladys T. McGarey
Eveline Horelle Daley

First printing: May 2013

All Rights Reserved.
No part of this book may be reproduced, stored in a retrieval system, or transmitted by any means, electronic, mechanical, photocopying, recording, or otherwise, without written permission from the publisher.

ISBN: 978-1-939625-31-1

Library of Congress Control Number: 2013908163

Published by Inkwell Productions
10869 N. Scottsdale Road # 103-128
Scottsdale, AZ 85254-5280

Tel. 480-315-3781
E-mail info@inkwellproductions.com
Website www.inkwellproductions.com

Printed in the United States of America

The World Needs Old Ladies

Index

Dedication ix
Acknowledgements xi
Forward xiii

Part 1 - THE ROOTS 1
  Chapter 1 - The Lecture 3
  Chapter 2 - Roots Of The Tree 9
  Chapter 3 - Discovering Our Roots 15
  Chapter 4 - Home In The Himalayas 23
  Chapter 5 - The Peacemaker 31
  Chapter 6 - She Was My Aunt Belle 39

Part 2 - THE TRUNK 49
  Chapter 7 - The Journey From The Head To The Heart ... 51
  Chapter 8 - Ancient Wisdom 55
  Chapter 9 - Imperfect But Growing 59
  Chapter 10 - The Gathering Of The Eagles 65
  Chapter 11 - Two Shawls 69

Part 3 - THE BARK 75
  Chapter 12 - Be Gentle When You Touch Me 77
  Chapter 13 - The Physician Within You 81
  Chapter 14 - The Gift Of Life 89

Part 4 - THE BRANCHES 95
  Chapter 15 - The Rocking Chair 97
  Chapter 16 - The Life Giving Power Of Humor 103
  Chapter 17 - Aging Into Health 107
  Chapter 18 - Who Am I 115
  Chapter 19 - Healthy Emotions 119

Part 5 - THE LEAVES ... 127
    Chapter 20 - The Importance Of Touch ... 129
    Chapter 21 - Consequences ... 133
    Chapter 22 - Food For Thought ... 139
    Chapter 23 - Communication ... 143
    Chapter 24 - My Healing ... 151
    Chapter 25 - The Aging Brain ... 159
    Chapter 26 - The Healing Power Of Dreams ... 163

Part 6 - THE BLOSSOMS ... 169
    Chapter 27 - Flowers Of Health ... 171
    Chapter 28 - Welcoming Consciousness ... 177
    Chapter 29 - The Garden ... 181
    Chapter 30 - Tools For Life ... 185

Part 7 - THE SEEDS AND FRUITS ... 191
    Chapter 31 - The Three Immortals ... 193
    Chapter 32 - Thoughts Are Things ... 197
    Chapter 33 - Pregnancy- the Disease ... 201
    Chapter 34 - Father Time, Mother Mature ... 207
    Chapter 35 - Growth And Change ... 211
    Chapter 36 - To Live Until We Die ... 219
    Chapter 37 - Old Mother Hubbard's Cupboard ... 225
    Chapter 38 - Mother Goose ... 237

Epilogue ... 243

Dedication

This book is dedicated to all of the Old Ladies of this world, past, present and future. Even Mother Earth is an Old Lady. All of life is dependent on us as we are dependent on the male energy. Such a beautiful balance of the Yin and Yang keeps life on this planet alive. The World does Need Old Ladies.

The World Needs Old Ladies

Acknowledgments

I wish to acknowledge Eveline Horelle Dailey, who helped me get my priorities cleared so that I could work on this book and who brought her own prospective to the work; Nick Ligidakis, our publisher, who kept prodding me for several years to do what I kept talking about, get my thoughts in to a book, and then took what we had and made it real; My daughter Helene, who has heard my thoughts all of her life and encouraged me to write what I lived; The rest of my children and grandchildren, who have given me so much to write about; Dr. Karilee Shames, who did a beautiful job of editing so that it came together as a real Tree of Life; Deedee McGarey my daughter-in-law, who took what we had done and polished and cleaned it so that it took on its own inner light; Doris Solbrig who did the final proof; Ravit Solomon, the graphic artist who took my pencil drawing and created the beautify cover ; The members of our study group who have lived with this growing project and kept encouraging us; My family of origin, who are my roots; Marie Grandstaff, who made the printing of this book a reality; My patients and friends, who have enriched my life so much that I have something to write about; And specially Don Dailey, Eveline's patient and loving husband, who

    loved her through all of this and gave those of us, who were part of their lives, the blessed opportunity to watch this beautiful love story unfold, and know that their love is still very much alive.

    Gladys Taylor McGarey

Foreward

I have been intending for several years to write a book about the unique gifts and perspectives that women of "years" have to offer the world. Its title, in my mind, has always been The World Needs Old Ladies - They Are The Tree of Life.

I had the information in my head and heart; I had much of it on paper, but life kept getting in the way of its becoming a book. One night, during one of the weekly study group meetings that I and a group of my "mature women" friends have, life shifted and I was inspired to ask one of the members for help. I, as an Old Lady who speaks and writes in American English filtered through my first language, which is Urdu, was delighted when she agreed to take on the task. Eveline is an Old Lady who thinks in French and writes in colorful English.

Old Ladies get ideas like this because they have lived a long time and they are not afraid to speak up and ask for help when need be. We know that not everything we say and do is original with us, but that it comes from what we have lived and experienced through many years. We bring these experiences and the experiences of others we have known with us to each new situation, and the blend engenders something unique and fresh. My thoughts have become "mine" because I have taken into my life and my world the richness of many relationships and experiences. I know that I do not "own" the thoughts I bring forth, but that they come through me to be shared with others.

My hope is that these thoughts will be further changed, reworked and clarified by you, the reader. Only then will they come to life and take root in your Tree of Life. The beauty of this process is that your Tree of Life will look very different from the one either Eveline or I have created. In much the same way every new life, by its very definition, is itself fresh and unique; therefore, a thought lives only as it continues to be part of change, only as it allows the stream of life to flow through it. Like the air we breathe, a breath only becomes our own when we take it in, use what we need, and release what we don't need. Just as we each must breathe our own breaths, we must also think our own thoughts, choosing what we need from what we discover.

As a title *The World Needs Old Ladies* could have sufficed, but the answers most of us seek are found only by examining the roots from which we come. A tree of life contains the essence of our humanity, and within its roots, its trunk, its branches, its leaves, its blossoms, its seeds and its fruits many cultures have found expression of the elements of our lives, including humor and pain. Although we discover this tree of life or its equivalent in most of the cultures of the earth, we do not discover any two of its leaves or fruits that are the same.

The Tree of Life is the metaphor with which we will work

in this book. It is fittingly part of our title.

So, dear reader, join us in our adventure. The roots of this tree go deeply into the earth and seem endless. They, like our thoughts, may be tangled, dry and broken in some places. They may be old and twisted, but they hold the tree steadily in the rain and the winds of time, nourishing its branches and shading the world. They, like Eveline and I, are Old Ladies who love and support all of life on earth and they have sustained us through many years. If we were to dig up a handful of these roots, we might be unable to trace them all the way to their original sources, but we can expose, gently, their contributions to life just as we, by looking at our accumulated experiences, can gently expose the changes in our lives that have made us who we are. Our roots will nourish us until we arrive at our final destination.

A tree's roots adapt as they may to the soil in which they grow. All parts of our tree, as our lives, are subject to change until like all living things, it makes its final transition.

The inner trunk of this metaphorical tree is its structural component, its framework. In the following pages the structural components of my life, my medical background and the Christian beliefs with which I grew up, will be blending with the artistic nature and heritage of both Eveline and myself. They will hold the endless concepts and experiences that have eventually accumulated as wisdom. It is this tree wisdom that is lifted through the structure of the trunk and into the limbs, leaves, blossoms and fruits by the sap. Within the sap flow the philosophies absorbed by the roots as it nourishes the tree with understanding, forgiveness, love, and patience. It sustains the limbs as they extend into the world, encountering stem cells, bacteria, and relationships with other life forms.

The blossoms and fruits on the branches are metaphors for our own sexuality, conception and the bringing forth of new life. The seeds are the products of our lives: our thoughts, our deeds, our children, our families.

Each one of us is special. We are given the gift of life supported by our roots, nurtured by the substance that is then transformed into our trunk, our bark, our branches, leaves, blossoms, and fruits. We are the fruits and the seeds from the Tree of Life itself. We are Old Ladies nourishing the future.

Eveline and I have chosen to mingle our thoughts and share them with you here. Please absorb what you find useful and bloom as you see fit.

Known the world over as the "Mother of Holistic Medicine", Gladys T. McGarey M.D., M.D. (H) asked me, Eveline, to write a book with her.

When it happened, I hesitated; she noticed, and told me to take some time to think it over. A moment passed, then I heard myself saying, "Yes. I can write something with you." I had no idea what that writing was going to involve or what ideas we would be presenting, but I trusted that it was going to work.

Dr. Gladys smiled and told me she had the title. When I heard "The World Needs Old Ladies," I took a deep breath, thinking of I am not sure what, but as I write these words I gain insight and I appreciate the honor that I have received as the greatest gift in my life. The world does indeed need Old Ladies. We are the roots of societies and we have experiences and wisdom to pass on to others.

As a retired physician, Dr. Gladys, may never have given a prescription with more authority than she did with that smile. I was going to collaborate on a book filled with the knowledge, astuteness, and gentle sense of comfort with humanity that I have come to know in her. I knew the type of medicine she practiced, and how she instructed her patients to be responsible for the development of their own wellness. This was an honor! I would be helping accumulate and present these qualities, sharing what she has gleaned from life and the Old Ladies around her. "Don't look so worried, I have plenty of material for you." She handed me a folder full of pages; some were typed, and others were handwritten. I am no better than anyone else when it comes to reading a doctor's writing, but I was flattered by her faith in me so, I took them home and decided to sleep on this mission, to see if a dream would give me some guidance. During the night, the moon and stars traveled, taking me to *The World Needs Old Ladies,* and by morning I found that the sun brought me an excited feeling as I began to explore The Tree of Life.

I, too, am an Old Lady, something that our western world has difficulty accepting, but the revelations of the morning were strong, honest and filled with a sense of adventure. During the course of our lives we accumulate experiences, and knowledge. We can share what we have accrued with younger generations in hope of making their journey easier, more prudent. I realized that morning that as an Old Lady I am freer to live my life and share my experiences as I choose.

I chose to venture to write a book with Dr. Gladys, one addressed to the younger women who will one day become the Old Ladies. It was natural to anticipate women's interest in our work, but I am intrigued by the interest it has generated in men. Apparently it is true that we all have a feminine side or at least an investment in a feminine perspective; at the very root of our being we are all connected. Or maybe it was due to shared stories like this:

A wonderful example of the worlds need for Old Ladies took place at the opening ceremonies of the 2012 Olympics. The world's best and strongest athletes were waiting to enter the arena, but they were unable to do so until a certain old lady made her appearance. No one was strong enough or talented enough to make an appearance before this old lady made hers. The Queen of England climbed into a helicopter, descended out of the blue into the arena, bowed to the world, and moved back into her place. Of course she could not have done it without the help of James Bond.

We Old Ladies need the strength of the men in our lives to do our work well. Still, many things in this world depend on us, on our stepping out of our expected roles to do the unexpected, then stepping back into our expected places. By the time we have mastered this dance, we have become Old Ladies, members of the oldest, strongest, most dependable underground movement the world has ever known. And most of the time we are not even seen.

I am here to help share the amazing stories and words of Dr. Gladys T. McGarey, a woman I have learned to love and respect, to cry and to laugh with. I have learned that as Old Ladies we are not afraid of humor; we can handle ridicule, and we know how to be serious when the need arises. What we have written here may be mystical, soulful, wise, healing, and compassionate; these are essential qualities of old ladies. You may not qualify for the title of Old Lady by means of your years, but, hopefully, as you read, you will be qualifying through the acquisition of wisdom.

Isn't life fun?

Authors' note to readers: To facilitate your reading, when Dr. Gladys writes, she will do so in italics.

The World Needs Old Ladies

PART 1
The Roots

Roots have been absorbing nutrients and giving life for eons. They hold together the earth as we know it and do so without being seen. Indeed, they hold and support the earth itself, intertwined and underground, they hold us upright as they nurture us. Without them we would have no trees and the earth would not support our lives. As members of the same system they are our conductors of life; they are responsible for our presence; we should take responsibility for theirs.

Roots teach the art of acquisition, for they search and find water, minerals and the nutrients needed to survive. They teach conservation: heeding the seasons, knowing the time to grow, the time to be dormant, the time to produce. They also know that, although there is a time they will no longer be active, they will continue to serve.

Our roots begin with our families, for within the human family, it is The Old Ladies that hold the wisdom we need.

The World Needs Old Ladies

Chapter 1
The Lecture

I was on my way to a lecture by Dr. Gladys T. McGarey; it was important to me. I already felt a connection to her by having read her books, but I needed to be in the same room with her, to listen to "The Mother of Holistic Medicine" with my own ears. Friends had told me some stories I simply did not believe and I was anxious to see if they were true.

It was a summer day in Arizona, hot and clear. On my way into the auditorium, I walked under a long line of trees that looked to be seventy-five feet tall. Noticing a sign at the base of one of them that read, "100 YEAR OLD PECAN TREES", I felt awe at the length of time they had lived. I knew that Dr. Gladys had not put in that much time, but I felt that both the trees, and what she was to talk about, would surely be of value to me.

The branches of these trees created an arch leading to the door of the auditorium. The shapes of green leaves crossed overhead, their shadows' fluttering shapes changing from almonds to sickles as they provided cover from the sun's rays. It was a breeze that moved them, making the glimpses of blue sky more intense, yet I did not feel any wind. The height of this arch, and the apparent strength of each branch, gave me a sense of safety and peace and the temperature here was more tolerable. The unfelt breeze teased my senses with a song, and a feeling of kindness enveloped me.

Above my head, branches were filled with pecans and the person walking ahead of me said the pecans would not be ready to harvest until October or later. I secretly hoped there would be another lecture in October, so I could return and reap a batch of pecans. A woman behind me must have read my thoughts, because she immediately volunteered that,"At this center it is allowed to harvest the fruits from mid-October until mid - November and there is always enough for everyone." I was quite surprised that people I did not know seemed to know what I was thinking.

I continued to walk into the small auditorium, a building that the architect Frank Lloyd Wright might have designed.

There was a scent of lemon and I noticed the ceiling beams; they had a luster perhaps created by lemon oil. The east wall was made of stained glass scenes representing a stylized garden. The north side, also glass, was clear and looked out on lush greenery.

Many speakers were advertised, but I was only interested in the Dr. McGarey. She was a pioneer, whose entire life was intriguingly unconventional. I found my seat toward the back of the room. Minutes later the room was full, and a gentleman took the podium.

BHUDI MA HAMARE GHAR ME ZAROOR HO

Curiously, the man behind the lectern had begun to talk

without any introduction. I had come to hear Dr. Gladys talk and I had the sensation that she was the reason for the words, but I did not understand them. I had very different expectations, all of which depended on understanding what was being said.

BHUDI MA HAMARE GHAR ME ZAROOR HO

Something I could not control was happening here. I had started the day unsure of what it would hold . Now, almost mid-day, the disturbing feeling had not left me. There was a force both inside and outside of me that appeared to have been driving me, and now this. What was this foreign phrase saying to me? I couldn't find a face in the audience that showed any comprehension. None of the women my age, none of the women who were older than me, and none of the men in the audience seemed any less confused than I was. There was a fair number of younger women here, too. If they were all searching for meaning as I was, what were we going to find through this gibberish? What language was that anyway?

I was confused, but receptive.

"Senseless you say, think again, come along, we are the Old Ladies. If you learn to cultivate these moments, you will enjoy the fine lines and the spaces between the words. That is a gift you will receive!" The man at the podium must also have sensed the reaction, but he extended his arms confidently toward the woman who had just spoken. She was Dr. Gladys.

She was certainly taking me by surprise. Why was she in the audience? How was it that she was only a seat away from me? What was she doing sitting in the middle row of the small auditorium! I did not expect her to be part of the audience, so I never saw her there. Dressed in a simple blue dress, she wore a silk shawl with purple and aqua designs folded around her shoulders. The luxurious silk was held together at the side of her left collarbone with a brooch that held her eyeglasses. The only sign that she was old was her gray hair. She wore it up in a chignon, with a braid around it and she had two small combs holding any stray hairs in place.

"The presence you have been waiting for, and the reason why you felt you had to be here, will be revealed. You may not agree, yet I know that older women everywhere in the world have these gifts to offer us. If you ever reach that station of your life, you too will have words to offer."

The loudspeaker spoke again!

BHUDI MA HAMARE GHAR ME ZAROOR HO

Now the man at the podium walked toward the audience, both arms at the ready to bring Dr. Gladys to the lectern.

Something sure and gentle about her commanded my attention. She cleared her throat. All eyes glanced toward her as the lecturer advanced.

"The language is Urdu; most of us on the western side of things do not speak Urdu. There are languages with something to teach us and I can give you an explanation to the sentence you keep hearing? Would you like one?"

The professor nodded in approval, and once more

extended his arms saying, "May I introduce Dr. Gladys T. McGarey." There was an explosion of sound in the audience as everyone applauded.

"Here is the basic meaning of the words you heard, Old Women need to be honored because wisdom blossoms among them; as the feet of the old ones makes the ground sacred, and they belong in our homes. All eyes were upon her. Perhaps the spectators were thinking of their grandmothers, or some other old woman they knew. They understood something, but they were not sure what it was. Without breaking the spell, she continued with a broader explanation. She had something to say, and she knew many things. Old ladies are like that!

"Older women, primarily because they have experienced the many sides of life, have long and strong roots. They have acquired wisdom, stored in their gut, heart, and in the pit of their stomach. Their juices are seasoned; they are centered, and ready to serve us." Before the audience could fully digest her words she she was centered behind the lectern. As she continued, I realized I had discovered what seemed to be a light that came from her mid- section, illuminating the rest of her. Soon the audience, too, bathed in that glow.

"I can tell you something else that may help you to better comprehend. It is from a neighborhood region of India where I was born, where some say,'It is most necessary to reside among elder women, and the other older ones, because the house needs this.'"

I could see signs of wonderment and amazement on the faces around me. Most people seemed to feel that we were the instruments being played, yet we were also the music.

The lecture ended, but I lingered in the courtyard. A large inviting tree, with twisted and exposed roots, was the perfect place to rest. The bark had caverns and highways, as bugs were making their way toward the light, escaping from the top. I needed to process all that I had heard, and most of all, I needed to understand how I felt.

Allowed to pause, without guilt, I realized that what I expected from this lecture was certainly different from what I was actually experiencing. It occurred to me then that my expectations of life might also need some revision. What was evident to me then was that my meeting with the doctor would not be a singular event.

Chapter 2
Roots of The Tree

I could not repeat what the doctor had said during the lecture, but I found myself reflecting upon the mysteries of life, sifting through the soil surrounding my roots. I had met people who were doing the same thing at the lecture, and there was something refreshing about their company. As we walked away from the auditorium we shared what we had learned.

One person said, " When people share what they know the load is lightened." She was an Old Lady. Another one told that our sharing gave us the nerve to continue on our path. Yet another Old Lady told me it was "the way," but she did not explain what that meant and without details or explanations I could only wonder about "the way."

Dr. Gladys had talked about the aging process. I had not thought yet not consider myself old, but with this lecture I began to get comfortable with the idea. I now call this comfort acceptance and these are some of the thoughts that encouraged it.

Knowledge and wisdom grow as we age. We are all duty bound to release the information acquired during a lifetime. We honor that which we uncover, and witness. Our roots hold our trunk, while our branches offer us balance. The blossoms that are born of us contain seeds of the future. And, in turn, they become the remedies of the ancient.

While it is true that I had not considered myself old, based on my life experiences I had accumulated some wisdom. That day, things I never considered I could share took shape in my mind. The idea that I was duty bound to release what I knew, seemed an order bigger than I could handle, yet I knew it was possible. If it is true that, "We are beacons and candles; a puff of the wind can blow us out," then there is no time to stumble if we are to accept the implied challenge underlying Dr. Gladys' words:

I accept the honor to talk for all the Old Ladies in the world. I am tired of hearing from women who considered themselves old and obsolete. No one is obsolete and the time is now for us to learn who we really are. Come out of hiding because you were scared, bushwhacked, or you simply did not dare speak. Your wisdom is needed.

That day, inside the small auditorium, the time was right to stand with staff in hand, and claim something fundamental to all older women. If it was Dr. Gladys' moment to talk, it was mine to listen.

We are the ROOTS, and this has always been so. We hold the soil of our earth. We started as a SEED, we became a STEM, from which we grew TRUNK, and branches. That took time, but then we grew LEAVES, and then we BLOSSOMED. We are the fruits, sitting here today. This is not the end of our journey; it is a beginning! We may have lost some of our leaves, standing naked in the wind for all to see. Out of this cycle we created the next generation, and we did so year after year, season after season and look around, we are still here. We are old, wrinkled, knotted and we are not considered pretty. We are here for you to learn from this is our gift to you. Women are the most alive underground movement in the world; no one seems to see us because we are quietly, constantly, and patiently doing our work. Even when we can no longer do what we thought we were here to do, we find that our job is as important and perhaps more important than before, because it is our roots that offer support to the rest. Even when the life force has dried up, a dead root still holds the earth together, and is the supporting structure. We are the memories, and the physical structure, as manifested by our very presence, not just in the lives of our offspring. There may come a time when we need to when we need to be cared for like we cared for our babies, but as long as we are here we are worth something. We are the wisdom, the lessons brought from the ground to teach, to support, to hold together.

My roots, although from a tree different than that of Dr. Gladys, reminded me that we were all part of a forest. I promised myself that I would learn more about trees and myself along the way. I was determined to find out more and I knew Old Ladies would guide me. I felt I had turned an invisible corner, and in one short afternoon my quest became clear; I too would become an Old Lady with something to say.

Not long after that afternoon, I became a patient of Dr. Gladys McGarey. Like the blossoms on a tree, our relationship changed, and we became friends.

Most cultures have knowledge of the symbol we call

"The Tree of Life". The tree, with its roots and branches, seems to speak to all of us. In cave drawings, the tree of life appears sketchy, perhaps because our ancestors had not yet discovered the fine arts, but they too understood the concept.

Strong enough to support the tree, the roots continuously work and grow to grace the earth. It is in relation to this symbol that Dr. Gladys recognizes the core truth of this book: that the world is in need of Old Ladies.

No life exists without many seasons; few escape the tempests of life. Trees withstand many storms, some may falter, then grow deeper roots, becoming stronger. At a time in my life when I thought I had lost everything, the desert tree taught me an important lesson. The tree in the Arizona desert, when it put its roots down, sometimes finds itself in a stone and sand combination called "caliche clay" which is almost like cement, forcing roots to grow through it. This would be a difficult task for any tree; and now it has two options. It can either spend all of its energy putting its roots out sidewise, in which case it dies, or it can instead concentrate its energy on its taproot. That taproot can steadily and consistently work itself down, through the caliche layers, until it finds the water it needs to survive. It can find the source of its supply.

Once the root has grown this far, the tree can rarely be knocked over. The root, the tree and its branches become very strong. A sort of marriage happens between Caliche that is calcium carbonate and other organic minerals and the root. The hard and the pliable opposites create a combination to survive the elements. Life itself seems to come with such combinations.

Ladies that have lived long enough to grow long taproots know the art of endurance. Because of it, they have plenty to say. Winds blow, storms come, droughts happen, but that taproot keeps the tree solid. I think during the years when I found myself in the most difficult situation of my life, I was able to allow my taproots to go deep enough to reach the source of renewal which was within me all along. I was then able to continue to go through life as the storms came and went. If I had put my energy into the surface roots (the superficial thoughts and events that presented themselves), the tap root would not have been able to break through the Caliche; and my tree would have fallen.

To me, the Old Ladies are the roots of the trees. They've come up as little shoots, spread their leaves and ultimately blossomed with fruits, and while people may not pay attention to the roots, we know that without those roots, none of the rest of the tree could survive. The older the tree, the stronger those roots are because they have gone through difficult times. They have broken through and have continued to grow and give life. It is in the processes of breaking new ground that they access wisdom and resources not available from the surface, wisdom that has been deep in the very heart of Mother Earth. Those are the roots that support the whole tree, the tree of life of the human family.

At my age now, the roots are still there. Though they are not always seen, they steady my feet and my arms, they strengthen what I have to say. At some level, we all know it is from the roots surrounding us that acquired substances, often made of hard rocks and soft tissues, make us who we are. When we are working with difficult issues, we often talk about the importance of getting to the root of the problem because none of us escape this fundamental truth. Roots, intertwined with science and humanity, will tell what they know, helping us to become aware of our own tree of life. It is under the shade of the trees, we bring life stories to you.

Albert Schweitzer said: "There can be no Kingdom of God in the world without the Kingdom of God in our hearts.

Chapter 3
Discovering Our Roots

At times life experiences can be difficult and we often feel worn out. But as we age, it is the survived experiences that enrich our world; they give us wisdom born of struggles and joys. The more we live, the more we learn to appreciate and understand life on its own terms. The Old Ladies are the keepers of such treasures, and they can find a place in our lives and homes.

Life also takes us on many journeys and we encounter a variety of people. Each encounter has the potential to give us something to use, something to grow with or from. We are marked and imprinted, with the subtle essence of those who have touched us and they, too, are changed by their contact with us. This circle of giving continues, offering a reservoir of lessons learned, and we can all draw from this place as needed. The beauty of this cycle and its process is that we can offer what we have learned to others. We may come from many trees, yet our deep roots are part of the same system.

I would like to share with you Dr. Gladys' introduction to the three "old ladies" who are largely responsible for the reservoir of lessons that have nurtured her life story. They are her roots and hearing her voice as she tells her stories may be the catalyst needed for us to find and nourish our own roots, to enable the plant coming out of the earth to bare the fruits by which we are to be remembered. Their lives have been involved in the field of medicine and, like many of us, their lives have impacted the lives of thousands of people. They are ordinary people who have lived extraordinary lives:

The first lady in my life is my mother who died at the age of eighty-nine, then my older sister Margaret, and my Aunt Belle. I use their lives and their stories as vehicles through which I can share concepts we have lived with, and therapies we have used.

I think every person alive has had, at some time in her life, an Old Lady who shared her wisdom. Surely, none of us would be here if some woman had not given us life. And, surely, we are all in this world together, all needing each other. Even the people we do not particularly like are here to enrich us, to teach us something. Much like a chair with four legs, the people we encounter are each in a different corner, supporting and keeping the balance. The four directions of our compass were perhaps created to hold us on our path Dr. Gladys, her mother, her sister Margaret, and her Aunt Belle are four solid pillars:

The four of us are very different women. The four of us are the roots of my tree of life. All of us are strong-willed women but we manifest it differently. Aunt Belle was pure fire and zeal. My mother embodied quiet, gentle humor in her strength. My sister Margaret is the essence of unconditional love, and she expresses it quietly and with gentleness. For me, I think it is my love for life itself that I express, and its not always quiet.

Understanding these women requires sorting out their

many twisted roots. They cannot offer their perspective without exposing the strength of these roots. I see it as tenacity, and they express it with resolve and enormous strength. Although, often what they express is an attribute of character they might not recognize in themselves.

Both Dr. Gladys and her sister Margaret were born in India, where they spent their childhood. They both became professionals in fields of medicine in the USA. Their mother and their aunt, were born in the USA, living as adults in India, where their medical professional work and life expression developed further. What is interesting to observe is that the four women went into similar fields of medicine and nursing, working together but separately toward the goal of healing humanity.

Two strong tap roots, one maternal (my mother), the other paternal (Aunt Belle), were the energies that sang to me.

Dr. Gladys talks about two with blue eyes and two with dark eyes, two contained their soul within wrinkled skin and two had smooth skin. Dr. Gladys did not inherit the blue eyes or the smooth skin, but these genetic variations lose their significance as people grow and learn to accept themselves as they are. Even though we come from the same seeds, learn that each of us is different. We copy those we admire; we learn from the examples they set for us and while learning we become teachers, even when our lessons have been hard ones. We walk on the roads that bring degrees of knowledge to us. It is "the way" as the lady at the lecture told me.

A good friend of Dr. Gladys addresses this concept as an artist would. Swiss born Elisabeth Kübler-Ross, a psychiatrist said, "People are like stained-glass windows. They sparkle and shine when the sun is out, but when the darkness sets in, their beauty is revealed only if there is a light from within."

I want to continue to get to know the ladies that were close to and part of Dr. Gladys's life. I want to learn how she developed her inner strength .

Her mother, Magdeline Elizabeth Siehl, was born of a German family in Cincinnati, Ohio, in January of the year 1881 on the 11th day. Those of you with interest in astrology may already know that an Aquarian woman is somewhat unpredictable; she has rules and they are her own. She is independent. She knows what is best for her. She is firm, inventive, and creative. This woman is a humanitarian, who enjoys interaction with people. She is wise.

My mother was called "Beth." She became a skilled seamstress and made fashionable blouses for sale. These blouses were works of art; they had tiny tucks and their design was original.

Her life was good, but there was more to explore. A new physician in her hometown of Cincinnati, Ohio, had healed a sick neighbor who had walked with a limp for many years. No medical doctor had been able to help her. Mother investigated and found that this new doctor was an Osteopath and she needed to know more about this form of healing. She wrote and was admitted to the Kirksville School of Osteopathic Medicine in Missouri. Off she went, following a call she did not yet understand.

Destiny has a way of placing us where we must be. In school, she met a student, John Calvin Taylor VI. He became her husband and in time my father. He was born April 9 1886, an Aries, a man full of surprises. He had a good balanced head on his shoulders and he did not like monotony. He was a man ready to take on the struggles of life, head on. India, with its mysteries and spices, called and with the support of the Reformed Presbyterian Church, he took his young wife and three-month-old son to Northern India.

My parents crossed the Atlantic Ocean and headed first for Bombay, now called Mumbai, on the banks of the Arabian Sea. WWI was in full swing and German submarines were all around in the oceans. They traveled with blackouts at night to a country they did not know, with a language they did not speak, and a culture very different from their own.

Once there, the first stop was a language school where they spent two years. The atmosphere in India was very different from that in Missouri. They first landed in a tropical climate, complete with monsoons from June to late September.

My mother and father learned to accommodate. This is something I have since mentioned often to patients, especially those with chronic disorders.

A thousand times she has told me to accommodate.

This young eager couple already knew about changes, and India offered plenty of opportunities for more. They traveled to Roorkee, in the United Provinces of North India, where they established a permanent residence for their family. Education being of great importance for the people of India, as it was for the Taylors, the family found Roorkee the perfect area. It is where the first steam engine traveled using the Ganges-Canal *as a route. Roorkee is also the home of the oldest technical institution in Asia. When the canal needed to be established for steam engines to go through, engineers were needed. India did what it could; they accommodated, and the first college to train the civil engineers that became responsible for this Upper Ganges Canal was established.*

Life continued as it does, and people do what they are called upon to do. In the case of the Taylors, the winter months were spent living in tents in the Indian jungles. There, they took their medical work, back, back, back into the jungle where they were desperately needed and where people with white skin were seldom seen. The Taylors spent one week in one village, then moved camp to the next one. People came from all over to receive the help they were offering.

In my first book, Lessons from the Lakeside, Dr. Gladys wrote a foreword. In it, she tells her father's story.

There was a time when father needed to go back farther into the jungle, traveling with his medical equipment. Coolies were part of his caravan, and they traveled for three days. On the fourth day, when he awakened, ready to move on, the coolies wouldn't move. They were sitting by the baggage but they were not about to move.

My father made attempts to persuade them to go further and faster, but he failed. This is when the lead coolie said: "Sahib, we have left our souls a three days journey back and we have to let them catch up to us before we move on." How often in our lives do we attempt to push people and ourselves beyond capacities?

At that point, my dad sat down, and waited all day. The

next day they moved on.

What a lesson this story has been for me! As I rush around in my busy life, I now remember that sometimes I simply must take time to let my soul catch up. If I do not, my body has a way of talking to me. "All right then, you will take time out!" I develop a problem often, a physical one, and I must stop. When we make excuses not to take the time to rest, we pay the price with our body.

When I saw Dr. Gladys as a patient, her very first prescription to me read REST.

The World Needs Old Ladies

Chapter 4
Home in the Himalayas

As Roorkee and the Himalayan Mountains became home, Dr. Gladys bonded to the people, the culture, the foods, and the very soul of India. After all, she was born in this land of extremes. She understands at multiple levels the poverty of humanity as well as she understands its riches.

These roots under her feet affect her because India is a part of her. The culture of her American missionary parents and the culture of India were the teachers of the lessons she learned and of the wisdom she acquired from all sides. The years of experiences and struggles in her own life are today gifts we joyfully share with you.

As we walk the roads of our lives we encounter many forks that demand we make a choice. I have learned to stop and ponder, knowing it is best to meet these junctions first with grace, then gratitude, and lastly with acceptance. When we reflect on the choices we have made, we will have the insight to see that we did the best we could with the abilities we had at the time. This is wisdom.

Let's visit some of the roads Dr. Gladys has traveled with family. Fourteen members of her family were able to visit with her the roads she had walked in India, to share more than the stories they had heard, to some of the influences that shaped their roots, to know some things unknown.

In 2006, around Christmas, I went to India with fourteen members of my family. We arrived at New Delhi airport, one of the largest and busiest in the world. We continued on to Dhera Dun, in northern India, to go up the mountain to Mussoorie and Landaur. This is where I went to Woodstock School, founded in 1854 for the children of missionaries in this part of India.

When I was a child, from our home, Landaur Villa as we called it, the visibility in was about 120 miles, over the plane to the south. The high Himalaya snow covered peaks were visible to the northeast and we encountered wildlife, migratory birds and an occasional leopard. The area was tourist-free when I was a child.

This time we traveled by bus, and I must say that travelling by bus in India, is still an adventure. It took us about an hour and a half to make the trip through hairpin curves from the level of the plains to the 7500 foot altitude. My family experienced a sense of adventure along with some goats and some chickens.

I clearly remember the trek up the same mountain in the 1920's, going from our home in Roorkee to Landaur Villa. In those days this trip took from early in the morning to late at night. It was one very full day!

From the time I was two years old until I was six I took this trip riding in a Kundi, which is a basket with a seat built into it. A coolie would lift this basket with me in its seat and strap it to his back. While he was facing forward, I was facing backward and I had the challenge to sit still as I puzzled this mystery and watched the world we had left behind, The coolie who was carrying me up a very steep and narrow path on his back was not a husky, muscular person. He was very slight, his legs and arms were very thin and he probably lived on one meal a day. He was really skinny and he did not look like a strong man. I learned that looks can be deceiving. He was all muscles and bones. This was the work he did, and had done ever since he was able to carry anything on his back, and I felt perfectly safe as I rode in this basket, looking down steep precipices, enjoying the view of the plains of India. If he had tripped or stumbled we both would have gone over the edge. He obviously never did.

My sister and younger brother were in similar Kundies, while my older brothers and my father were hiking alongside. My mother rode in a Dandi which is like a sedan chair that is carried by four men. Other coolies carried our luggage which often consisted of very heavy trunks.

Even as a small child, I wondered how these men could do this work. I knew that my brothers, who looked much stronger and were more muscular, could not begin to carry such loads even for a short distance. How did these men carry people and heavy things all day long all the way up the mountain? It didn't make sense. My brothers ate much more than these men. So how could they be so strong?

I have learned a few things in the intervening years and one of them is that real strength often manifests in unexpected places. Big muscles may not be as efficient when doing the work these coolies do. Every cell in their bodies uses every molecule of nutrition efficiently. Their bodies waste nothing. They know the importance of breathing properly, balancing the load, and lifting it in the right way.

It is important for us to look for strength and balance in unexpected places. It is important for us to use the nutrition available to us physically, mentally and spiritually, wasting nothing. It is important for us to understand that our very life depends on each breath we take. Keeping the air breathable for all living things becomes essential to life itself as is proper balance in our lives.

Among the fourteen members of the group was Dr. Rev. Barbara McGarey, Dr. Gladys's daughter-in-law. Overwhelmed by something she was not prepared for, though she had heard stories and had seen pictures, she had to write her feelings in a way we can share here. She had to tell in her own words what was unfolding all around her:

> Landaur Villa is as exotic and beautiful as
> the name may sound. It is a bungalow perched,
> literally on the edge of the mountain.
> From its porch, which extends around it, you can
> see all of the Hill Station of Mussorie. At
> 7,500 feet, you are truly in the clouds. To
> the East, rising above the mists of the
> mountain valleys, are the high Himalayas.
> Their ridges at a great distance in another
> country still dominate the sky as you look
> east. What an amazing awesome view.

Did we dance there? Not in the literal sense of the word, dance. But we stood there with Gladys and Margaret and as they walked around their childhood home we heard story after story, "Oh look! This is where..." And this went on and on binding them to a time before, and us to them and to that time as well. We were blended into another place.

Momma's desk and the table where they all sat and did their work is still there. The chest that had been in the living room was still there with dishes inside from another owner. It stood as it always had, tucked in the corner, richly colored wood. All of this is so beautiful.
Then they stood and looked where they had played as girls with their brothers. "This is the tree, isn't it, where Dad hung the swing?" They looked up. We looked with them and saw across the branch a rusted piece of metal and links of chains around it. The metal had been placed over the branch to protect it and it had. The chains with five links on each side of a branch were rusted but, as we looked, we saw it bright and shiny, with young children gleeful around the base seeing the swing

for the first time and taking turns to see who could swing out the farthest. It must have been a glorious swing that took them out over the patio and the house. They were girls then, and in this moment are girls again. So that was the dancing. Not a two-step or ballet but a whirling dance of the heart unlike any other.
OH look! Come see! This is where.

Dr. Rev. Barbara McGarey was probably transformed because she walked where not a sage walked, but where her mother-in-law pointed moments of her youth.

A tree with strong roots grows strong feelings and there are times in our lives when the simple beauty of nature and of humanity is meant to overwhelm us. It is that distinctive feeling Old Ladies manage to teach when we pay attention to them.

Sometimes I wonder what went wrong with us, the sentinels of this planet? Have we forgotten our places in the greater scheme of things? I trust that the fourteen members of Dr. Glady's family wanted to capture the part of their personal history that they knew was attainable. While we watch the news, read the papers on our latest device, we forget who we are, what we are, or forget our own potential. Let us not forget our obligations as the keepers of roots.

Another mystery I have pondered during this writing process is how those men in my trips up the mountain could be so willing to carry other people's baggage. I knew it was their job and they clearly accepted that it was their job doing it with efficiency. Haggling was also apparently part of the package since it went on every time. It was not because they felt they would be cheated out of a regular price; it was something that added a little spice to the work that they were doing. They always asked more than they expected and sometimes an unsuspecting person would pay it. In India, everyone understands that's the way it is and it seems to enrich everyone's overall experience.

I think it is human nature to add more interest to a job whenever we can, evidenced by the infinite creativity we devote to it. With regard to carrying another person's baggage for a period of time, mindful interest has certainly enriched my job as a physician. Every time I got into the kundi, the coolie and I became one unit. I was totally dependent on him and it was important for me not to wiggle. My job was to not throw him off balance, and his job was to get me to my destination safely. We both approached our tasks with focused respect. For the period of time that I was being transported from one place to the next, we were totally bonded together. The straps that held the basket on his shoulder and the strap to hold the upper part of the basket around his forehead were also strong and dependable. It was however, the living spirit of the man himself that made the job possible. We had to respect each other and it created an aspect of love between us. We were not conscious of it, but it was there then.

And so it is in my work as a physician. The physician needs the patient and the patient has need of a physician for a period of time. When the two are working together during this time a bond of love is created.

Throughout our lives we have mountains to climb. This means both going up and coming down. We don't climb these mountains alone. Life demands that we find ways in which to climb them together. It may mean riding backwards on the back of another human being. But oh, the view we get and the life experience that is shared!

Life is so full of unexpected wonders and great expansive views.

Chapter 5
The Peacemaker

When I think of the Taylors I can only imagine what incredible stories the family tells. I know only a few. I know their presence in India was full of adventures, but that the reason for their presence was service. In all of their actions they touched not only those they came to help but also many they never met.

Summers in India are humid and hot, and August of 1918 was no different when my sister Margaret was born. She was the middle child in our family, with two older brothers, my younger brother and me, Margaret was the peacemaker. Always fair, patient and peaceful, in her presence people felt loved and cared for. At home she was the one that divided the pumpkin pie we had on special occasions.

In school, she was so soft-spoken that the teachers had her on the first row in order to hear her answers when asked a question. Margaret was shy by nature. Me, I was the one placed in the back of the room; even when I whispered the teacher could hear me.

Sets of sisters close in age are often quite different. This certainly applied to us. Margaret was the older sister who accepted me with all of my noise, my opinions and my excitement.

Margaret was poised; I made the noise. Without getting angry she was able to stand her ground, and I had to accept who and what she was.

This was a strength that served her well. She learned early to accept life on its own terms, but when she decided on anything, she did it with consciousness and she was able to stand up for herself quietly without being confrontational. She was clear about her ideals and lived by them. If situations around her became difficult or didn't measure up to her life purpose or ideals she removed herself and continued with what she needed to do. She was simply more gracious and accepting than I could ever be.

An event between us occurred one time after we had returned from a trip to the United States, I was twelve and Margaret was fourteen. I had been invited to a birthday party. In the United States Margaret had purchased a pair of black patent leather shoes, something impossible to get in India. I begged, pleaded, pleaded and begged until she let me borrow her shoes. I wore them to the party and while there, I forgot how precious the shoes were to her. I played all sorts of games and scuffed the shoes. When I came back home, her beautiful patent leather shoes were scuffed and no longer pretty. Margaret cried because I had ruined her shoes. She was sad and disappointed in me. Her big blue eyes full of tears looked at me, not condemning me, not spiteful ; her wordless response was harder than if she had screamed, yelled or thrown something at me. I had hurt her and her reaction made me conscious of what I had done. I never forgot that feeling.

At seventeen she went to the United States to begin her college education. This was a foreign place with a different culture ,and things were uncomfortable for her. Neither women nor men dressed as they did in India, and the interests of American college girls were at odds with most of her values. Perhaps Margaret, with her sense of tranquility was ready to take on the world. She had learned to cope by listening to what was said, considering issues carefully and responding thoughtfully, and she didn't allow herself to be pushed aside or trampled on.

She never failed to realize how different she must seem and from personal experience, I understood her dilemmas. When I came to the United States from France, I also had to face a new world, new ideas and new ways of life. The language, the culture and the foods most people ate were different than those to which I had grown accustomed. My first moments upon my arrival in the USA were uncomfortable. It was in sea of people, all different than I, all speaking in a tongue I had not heard. Unable to understand anyone, I was uncomfortable and a little afraid. Fortunately, by seventeen I knew that fear and discomfort are temporary maladies. I went to a school where young men and women did not understand me any more than I understood them, and this very fact made my inability to speak English less terrifying. Time passed quickly and soon we had all learned enough to understand each other.

The difficult moments of our lives are gifted to us, and we learn resilience from them. We know a challenge is little more than a new adventure, a passing moment. At seventeen Margaret and had I encountered such a wide variety of different experiences that we were sufficiently resilient to survive our encounters with the differences we found in the States

My sister's way of teaching me and living around me impacted me to the core. It was never the things she said but the way she lived that held me in check. In our family, we have all grown to love, respect and understand her.

I am fortunate to have had Margaret in my life; she is the kind of Old Lady we all need to know. The presence of such people bless us and they are not diminished by the gifts they offer us. Their unassuming ways of being and of living their lives are the kind of examples most able to influence us. Those of us lucky enough to be around such steady people grow and learn lessons in ways that we never can forget.

Margaret seems to instill in others a tranquil feeling. She is a person that knows no fear; she does not seem to perceive fear the way most of us do. As a religious person, she attributes this gift to "Perfect love casteth out all fear."

One icy, cold morning she went to the post office. As she was coming out she saw a horse in distress attached to a buggy. His master, an Amish man, was nowhere to be found. The horse had been tethered to a post but somehow had gotten loose. He was struggling on the ice and his hoofs were slipping. Margaret called to somebody in the post office but nobody heard her. She approached the horse, and began speaking softly to this large, strong animal, steadily reaching between the horse's legs as it continued trying to catch some semblance of balance. Taking and holding the tether, she continued to talk peacefully as she pulled tighter and tighter. Eventually she was able to tie him to the post and once the horse had no reason to be frightened, he settled down. Margaret went back to the post-office and told the people there what had happened. They got in touch with the Amish man who was across the street and hadn't realized that anything had gone wrong.

Margaret had not grown up with horses, but she recognized in his eyes that he was consumed with fear. I asked her, "How in the world did you know what to do?" She said, "I don't know, I saw fear, talked to him and once the tether was in my hand somehow I did what I was able to do. I don't know how I did it."

Could it be, when we fear, we can either be paralyzed or go on high alert, as in fight or flight? If we can recognize this emotion, and softly cast the fear away, at that point we are able to do what we need to do. Little acts of kindness are quite possible when there is no fear.

Margaret continues to live in New Wilmington, Pennsylvania, in the heart of an Amish community, in a house her husband had built after he retired. Though he died when she was eighty-two, she decided to remain where she was comfortable with memories, in a town she loved.

For years I talked to her about moving to Phoenix, Arizona to be near me. I had my plans ready to execute. An additional room could be built for her. It would be attached to my home but she still would have her own space and we could both live out our years that way. I expected that Margaret would say that she would think about it, and I would give her the proper time to think about it but I would continue to push her to think about it. I even suggested she move out for part of the year, maybe during *the winter.*

Years later, when I was visiting her, I realized she had created a life for herself in this small town. She was essential to the community she had created. For the first time in her life, she was alone, but she was not lonely. She had made friends, and was accessible to people when they needed her. When she entered a room, she brought peace, hope and love.

She has a habit when she takes her mile and a half walk everyday: if she sees what does not belong, she picks it up and she puts trash where it belongs. She told me a story about finding a six-pack of beer on the side of the road. She picked it up, brought it home and disposed of it instead of leaving it on the side of the road. I suggested that maybe someone had stashed it there and intended to come back for it; to this she replied, "They should have found another place to stash it."

My older sister Margaret is an extraordinary person, who has no need to talk about who she is or what she does. When she climbs on her tractor to mow the grass or take care of the snow, she does it the best way she can. She is also a recycler, not because it is a word en vogue, but because she sees the utility of things. The wax paper out of her box of cereal is saved and used when she needs wax paper, but she keeps an uncluttered home with no unnecessary possessions.

From my mother she learned to plant. Her flowers bloom when they are supposed to, her plants grow in the most unexpected ways. Unlike me, she has not written any books. She is a nurse who told me I might make a good doctor but I would make a lousy nurse. Margaret is always right!

There is an inner peace about her and that is something that permeates her life and spills over onto the rest of us. She prays every day for all her nieces and nephews, and there is a multitude of them. Their names are listed in a prayer inventory that is checked every day and there is something to be said about the power of prayer from Aunt Margaret. Struggles are part of life and they are given to us to teach us something we did not know or did not learn well. Some of us encounter these times alone but some of us are aware of thoughts and prayers of others. When we feel supported, we gain confidence, we become less vulnerable, and less fragile, making it easier to learn from our difficulties. When one of her nephews was going through a rough time he said, "Well, at least I know Aunt Margaret is praying for me every day."

Ours is a lucky family to have an Aunt Margaret, one of the many angels able, with her quiet strength, to support people, be they in a garden club, a church choir or a sewing group. I have been in the presence of Margaret and I have long been in her prayers and can affirm that in that Old Lady, one finds a sense of calm and a compassionate glow. On our Tree of Life she keeps the branches healthy and the blooming.

I wanted to grow my tree in perfect sequence, each branch was to be symmetrical, they each needed to reach out to the sky at the same time and they each needed to be the perfect length. Few trees or people are ever symmetrical.

It was an Old Lady who came to my rescue as we talked about the ages of our children and how different they were. She had lost two of hers and I had two who had grown to adulthood.

My friend looked at me a while, as only Old Ladies can. "Well dear, I suppose you know, when it comes to family, the way they grow is unique; they each have their own attributes. They grow differently even if they came from the same roots. I think your doctor Gladys understands this and you are not exactly there yet. In a few more years, you may understand that life does not arrive in a symmetrical package. Things happen in their own time; their duration is not of your control. You are still a youngster. Go play in your garden and you will see that your plants will grow only as they need to. People are like that too.

Chapter 6
She Was My Aunt Belle

Lorenna Belle Taylor Stout was born on a farm on a warm August day in Manhattan, Kansas. She was my father's younger sister. She followed in his footsteps and studied osteopathy under Dr. A. T. Still, as he did. Following her older brother, she too went to India as a missionary in 1922. After about five years, she separated from the United Presbyterian Church's Mission Board.

She was planning to move to Northern India but one morning before her departure workers from the mill came to the mission with a package in their arms. When they handed it over to Aunt Belle she found a newborn baby girl, whose parents, because they had wanted a boy, had thrown her away in a cactus patch. The police had already refused to take her in, but when the mill workers took her to Aunt Belle the baby found a home. It takes more than an open heart to take in a baby from a cactus patch, raise it, and become the channel for a better life for it. It took more than two hours to pick the cactus thorns from the baby's little body. She developed pneumonia, and for two months no one knew whether she would live or not.

She did live, and Aunt Belle adopted this cactus baby,

naming her Dorcas Anandi. She became the love of my aunt's life and perhaps she was the catalyst that got my aunt to Northern India where our family lived.

My parents had also taken in abandoned children and Aunt Belle worked with them to create a home for the children of lepers. She returned to the USA in 1939 and married a Pentecostal minister named Edward Stout, but the work that Aunt Belle began continues to serve children of lepers today. They are still considered the "untouchables", although they themselves may not have leprosy.

It must have been wondrous for Dr. Gladys to grow up around such remarkable people. Her Aunt Belle felt a need to help anyone in need. When I read about her, or listen to the stories about her, I recognize an amazing woman, unafraid to do the things she felt called to do. Coming from the same roots, Dr. Gladys has many of Aunt Belle's attributes.

After twelve years of marriage, Aunt Belle's husband Ed died and she returned to India, to Bhogpur, which is where the first home for children of leper parents is located. A new energy grew, her work expanded, and she and the children had a home, one created with no visible means of support. They depended entirely on small donations from people who had heard about her work and what she and the children could grow on the property. Aunt Belle never sent anyone away; there was always room for more even when there was no money or room. At this writing, the home for the children of leper parents still exists in Bhogpur.

Aunt Belle was ninety-one when she came back to the United States for the last time. She traveled on a Greyhound bus, visited friends and churches throughout the country and lectured. Everyone who heard her was inspired by her words and even today, I hear from people I do not know who have been inspired by Aunt Belle. They carry with them her dedication, clarity of vision and the purity of her spirit.

After this, her last visit to the United States, Aunt Belle returned to India, where she died a year later and was buried in Jeetghar. There is no mausoleum to mark her passing, only a humble slab marks her grave. The people in Jeetghar and surrounding areas have made it into a shrine.

It is easy for our fear to paralyze us, but Aunt Belle's courage is an inspiration to action. Knowing how fearlessly she gave of herself, we can all be inspired by the courage it took her to follow her bliss.

There are unwritten and unseen laws which give energy to the choices we make. Aunt Belle must have known about these laws because she had the faith to give her attention where it was needed and to follow her ideals. Her faith and these laws opened her to great ideas, helped her to achieve what she was called to. Although we now live in a world filled with statistics, in the larger scheme of things it is not the numbers that count, it is the actions that have the capacity to impact individual lives. Aunt Belle was one of those women able to recognize opportunities and act upon them. She was not afraid to follow the faith that guided her.

As we get older we realize that each person we meet is a potential teacher. The more I observe the world around me and its older women, the more I find that they are able to take on challenges that seem insurmountable. Aunt Belle was able to shelter, love and care for hundreds of children during the course of her life. She did what she believed to be necessary. She did it without formal funding, but people would hear about her work and spontaneously send her money.

She had a direct connection to Jesus. When I was fifteen years old I was staying with her a while. One night I saw her on her knees with a single Pisa in the palm of her hand. This Indian coin, the smallest value usable in the country, was all she had. She was confident, not at all desperate as she said, "These are your children. I'm taking care of them but I don't have any more money. I need to be able to buy food and clothing for them; I need to take care of them. They're your children. Please, I need this money." I remember times, when there was a special bill to be paid, Aunt Belle would give Jesus an exact amount and, low and behold, the next day that money would show up.

In 1969, I was with a group of people on a trip around the world, and we planned to visit the places where I grew up. We stopped to visit Aunt Belle in Jettghar where she had just opened a new home for the children. Arriving after a drive up a winding road, I noticed there were some young boys building something. I asked Aunt Belle about it and without ceremony she told me they were building a cow shed. "Oh, I didn't know you had a cow." Full of surprises and unshakable faith, she replied, "Well, I don't, but if I build a cow shed, God will supply the cow." When the shed was completed a cow did appear at the front gate of the compound. We don't know where the cow came from, but it supplied the children with the nutrition they needed and provided the home with the milk to make things like yogurt and paneer, an Indian cheese dating back to 6,000 BC.

Aunt Belle lived by the words of her Bible. If she had a decision to make, she would pray about it, open the book and discover a verse that would be her guiding words.

It was in this way that, in 1939, my aunt decided it was time to return to the United States. She knew she was supposed to go through Afghanistan and eventually to Germany. Her hope while there was to get an audience with Hitler; she wanted to convert him. Obviously this was not a mission she was able to accomplish, but she did get to Latvia in the Soviet Union. By then the Molotov Ribbentrop pact between the Soviets and Germany had changed the sphere of influences and it was time to go home to the United States.

There were things that even Aunt Belle found she could not do. They did not prevent her from doing all that she could. As I write one thing becomes clear: the Aunt Belles of the world are needed. They are the Old Ladies who, by their actions, teach us that we, too, can find the faith and the courage to follow our hearts.

In order to become the Old Ladies, teachers and caretakers of the future, we must be courageous enough to experience our lives as fully as possible. This is the collecting time of youth and even our follies and indiscretions hold lessons to to be shared. A life well lived gives us the gifts we have to offer later in our lives.

My brother *Carl had become a physician and a professor at John's Hopkins Hospital Medical School in Baltimore, MD. He and his son, Daniel together created an NGO entitled*

"Future Generations", and worked with health issues around the world. It may have been an afternoon of 1970, when Dan was reminiscing with two of his friends. These two friends of Dan's were fellow mountain climbers and the three of them had conquered the highest mountains in the world. They began to share a story from their youth. It was 1939, they were at the Khyber Pass, ready to cross to Afghanistan when a woman showed up and told them God had directed her to accompany them. Women were not allowed to travel by themselves in Afghanistan and knowing that, though they thought the idea fascinating, they were not at all interested in taking her along. No matter how they attempted to avoid her, there she was. She knew where they were at all times and they were not going to escape. Hoping to leave her behind, they decided to leave very early in the morning, before she showed up again. To their surprise when they got to the car she was there with her small suitcase, ready to go with them. Thus she managed to have them escort her through the entire Afghan country, after which she continued on alone to Europe. This unknown woman was of course, Dan's Aunt Belle. When she got a message from God, no storm or catastrophe could stop her from at least attempting to complete the task she felt she was given.

When Aunt Belle returned to the United States she arrived with no money, only the clothes on her back and a few things in a ragged suitcase. She stayed with her sister, my Aunt Mary, who resided in Washington, D.C. Mary insisted on buying new shoes and clothing for Belle, but one day Aunt Belle came upon a woman with shoes that were in very bad shape, whereupon she decided to trade shoes with the woman and returned home wearing the woman's beat-up old shoes. When Aunt Belle explained she was so blessed that when she saw someone who was not, she had no choice but to give what she had, in this case it was a pair of shoes. Aunt Mary's consternation did not last.

Aunt Belle was giving me some advice one day. In a prayerful position, her hands together, the right hand fingers were a little higher than the fingers on the left hand; she said, "Gladys, don't ever forget, when the Lord is working like this," she wiggled her right hand fingers, "remember He is always a little bit ahead."

Through the years those words came back to me. Whenever I was experiencing difficult times, when I felt everything was against me, despite my doing the best that I could, I thought of her fingers and the thought of them always led me to the idea that light overcomes darkness.

Aunt Belle created loving homes for those deemed untouchable. It was because of the great need and not because the jobs were easy that she and my parents kept taking in children of leper parents. I can still hear her talking about the barriers societies too often place on them and their communities. She frequently drew strength from her idea that "easy jobs are done by those who can, hard jobs are done by those who try, and impossible jobs are done by those who care." It was work that did take courage, but courage doesn't always roar. At times, it is the still small voice at night that says, "I will try again tomorrow."

Thus, it became the goal to have homes for them, to provide an environment filled with love, with normalcy. These children *learned to accept themselves for who they were: beloved children of a loving God, not "children of lepers", as their environment labeled them. There are now thousands of people who are high functioning adults because of the homes and schools that were created for them. They reside around the world and the work that began decades ago continues today. Some of those children are now doctors and nurses, educators, and merchants.*

Dr. Gladys returned from one of her trips to India with saris and stories. This one about Roni is worth retelling.

Born of parents who were lepers, his full name was Roni Saurahb Massih. Dr. Gladys, who speaks Hindustani, simulated a good Indian accent when she reported her conversation with Roni:

"Gran Ma, thank you for coming back, we need you, I will help you examine the 900 children from the homes; but Gran Maji, we need a good dentist here like your brother John. I need to go to school. Grand Maji, can your foundation send me to dental school. When I come back from school, I will start a clinic."

During the course of our lives, and especially as we grow into awareness of our surroundings, we notice unfortunate souls walking the earth. This recognition, however, does not always bring a response. At times, awareness and action seem disconnected and we veer toward inaction, hoping to avoid painful circumstances. We are presented with opportunities for accomplishment; we are offered pathways to do what we judge we need to do. The idea is not to fool ourselves into apathy, but to use our hearts and awareness in the name of love. I did just that and I followed an inner guidance, knowing that my part was to do the best I could to send this young man to dental school.

Opportunities to do the unimaginable came knocking at my door; I found myself raising funds to send one of the children to dental school and Roni became a good friend.

Sadly, Roni did not finish dental school; he, along with his brother, was killed in a car accident. How he studied, or for how long, was out of my control. Roni's life exemplified what a human being can do when minds and hearts focus on what needs to be done. With anything in life, there are no guarantees and I feel as a human being, walking toward something I have never seen that I must take the steps which may, or may not, lead me to full understanding. In the town of Bhogpur, Roni's parents still care for over 300 children of leper parents. There is not yet the dental clinic Roni dreamed of.

PART 2
The Trunk

By the design of the master gardener, the trunk of a tree provides support for the branches, and the multitudes of leaves, blooms, seeds and fruits that will grow from them. It contains the complex system that allows the tree to function as it does. Similarly, in humans the numerous people we meet, the experiences we continuously have and have accumulated, combine to support us and allow each of us to function as uniquely as the individual tree trunks in a forest. Our social structures and experiences shape the place where our feelings and our heart reside. The trunk of the tree holds, transports and distributes the sap of life, much like our societies hold, transport and distribute our value systems and moral structures. These substances, not always seen, can be found dead or alive inside the trunk, and within the social structures that shape our lives.

A trunk, a society, is a way station, transferring knowledge, insights, support, shapes and strengths from its roots to its branches. Each has many layers, and grows many branches, without which its fruits could never be counted.

The lives of old ladies contribute to and resemble such a trunk.

The World Needs Old Ladies

Chapter 7
Journey from Head to Heart

In William Sloane Coffin's book, <u>Credo</u>, he says:

"The longest and most arduous trip in the world is often the journey from the head to the heart. Until that round trip is completed, we remain at war with ourselves. And, of course, those at war with themselves are apt to make casualties of others including, friends and loved ones."

When I think about this statement, I realize that many of the systems with which we work have lost their connection to the heart, and now focus almost exclusively on the mind. Missing the heart is a serious omission in any system relating to beings with hearts. It is especially serious in the system I am most involved with: the broken healthcare system. There are many physicians and other practitioners who find themselves working within this system in which a paradigm shift is vital.

It seems to me that, since World War II, healthcare has been directed completely by a cold intellect; so much of its attention has been focused on repairing the physical body that the emotional health of the human heart has been denied its share, has been neglected. Medical students are not being taught about the importance of that trip from the head to the heart.

I was talking to a senior medical student recently. She is going to be starting her residency in obstetrics and gynecology. That morning at Grand Rounds, she had presented the case of a family she had been working with for the last three months. The family, upon discovery that their unborn baby had congenital deformities, had decided to continue the pregnancy. At thirty-one weeks the baby died en utero, and this young medical student was with the parents as the baby was delivered two days later. She felt her job was to be supportive of the parents through the emotional and deep spiritual pain they were facing. As she described the experience at the Grand Rounds, her focus was entirely on how the parents had felt. She talked about how they had coped with the whole pregnancy, and how their grief and pain was her primary concern.

As she ended her report, the attending physician asked her if the baby had a harelip. The medical student was at a loss to answer because she had not focused on the physical aspect of the dead baby, but had focused all her attention on the parents' needs as the baby was handed to the mother, professionally wrapped, with most of his body concealed.

Clearly, to this student the physical aspects of the delivery were secondary to the emotional, heartfelt life loss that the parents were experiencing. The attending physician's comments were that the student had not done her work well because her focus was on the "heart'" matters of the situation rather than the appropriate physical pathology.

Our medical systems are so focused on pathology at a physical level that is it very hard for us to include this spiritually vital journey from head to heart.

An Old Lady is speaking to us; let us listen to the real story being told. When we talk to a person, let us engage mentally in nothing else. Let us focus on the person. Let doctors of medicine do the same. Let the paradigm shift start with each individual, with us. It is not impossible, it is not difficult. It does take practice, awareness and sometimes a touch to be totally focused on each person with whom we interact, but focus we can on living, rather than dying.

The cells of our body know their jobs. We, as living human beings, set our ideals and work toward the manifestation of the fruits of our spirit and our cells know what to do.

In the 1980's, Robert Becker, MD., in his groundbreaking book, <u>The Body Electric,</u> *wrote about the use of electrical impulses to stimulate re-growth of limbs in frogs, and even rats. He likened the electrical impulse that he used to the electrical impulse that is created through a nerve within the human body which stimulates a cell to do what it is structured to do.*

Let me tell you the story of a dear friend who manifested this principle. After a severe injury in a devastating automobile accident, she fractured two cervical vertebrae and one thoracic, so that she was placed in a neck and upper body cast, able to move only her eyes and mouth. She had to lie on her back, unable to turn her head and all she had to look at was the ceiling above her bed. She was told that probably she would be unable to walk for the rest of her life and that chances of repairing the damages were very slim.

When I saw her, we talked about the possibilities of the

body cells regenerating. I told her about Dr. Becker's work, explaining that there were bone cells called osteoblasts and osteoclasts that do reconstructive work. One takes away the debris and clears up the area, the other regrows bones cells and reconstructs the bones.

She understood this at multiple levels, and began with her mind to reconstruct the bony tissue in her spine. Since she is an artist with amazing creativity, she healed quickly. Within three months she was sitting up, and within six months she was out and about with only a soft brace on her neck.

Now completely functional, she has entered into a marriage, of mind, heart and the divine spark. She has been able to reconstruct her spine and rebuild her body.

In the Bible it is said: "As a man thinks, so is he." Our thoughts are things and evolving research is giving us the tools with which we can manifest this basic principle in our lives.

Science, as it joins hands with the divine, is able to accomplish what we deem impossible. In matters of living medicine, there is a marriage between patient and the spark of life, which is an electrical impulse. These principles reside well tucked away within our being, in the trunk of our tree of life. Many Old Ladies have become aware of this healing and are thus able to contribute to the loving energy that allows this type of healing to happen.

Chapter 8
Ancient Wisdom

Our lives take us where we need to be. Wish and think as we may, we are not in control; things change without our permission and we can never know what will trigger that change. Change is difficult for all of us but it gets easier if we can be open to it. Unanticipated experiences teach us acceptance and as we grow, we learn to be less attached to having the ideal set of circumstances, accepting what we have and doing the best we can. Our life improves when we are able to take it one step at a time. When we falter or bruise our knees, it's good to remember that we can always get up and continue our journey in a new direction if necessary. We have the innate strength to accomplish what is best for us, but we need to be open to new pathways. Our feet will take us in any direction we chose.

While ideas are located in our mind, our ideals are snugly nestled in our hearts; the rhythm between the two can be felt in our chest. Ideas may link minds, but it is the ideals that link hearts. Either way, the effects that one life has on another involve both idea and ideals; the neglect of either aspect of connection renders the experience incomplete.

I remember, as a child in India, being called away from

the breakfast table one morning because a snake charmer was in the front yard. He told us he had a cobra in his basket that he had caught the night before, and he asked my father if he would like to see it. My father, curious by nature, agreed readily, and the snake charmer told us all to stand back. Indian snake charmers remove the fangs of the cobra in order to decrease the danger of working with them but this new snake had not been treated and was therefore quite dangerous. The snake charmer put the basket containing the cobra in front of him, picked up his gourd flute, called a been, and as he lifted the lid of the basket, simultaneously began to play the flute. Quick as a flash, the cobra was a good ten or fifteen feet away from him, but as soon as the first notes escaped the flute the cobra stopped, turned himself around and came back to stop right in front of the snake charmer's knee, where he raised himself up, opened his hood, and began to weave back and forth gently, as if hypnotized by the music.

When the snake charmer finished, he started to put down his flute, to throw the blanket over the snake and to put him back into the basket, but the snake struck, and bit him on the index finger. The snake charmer proceeded to wrap the cobra up in the blanket and get him into the basket. My father, a physician, started to initiate some emergency measures, but the snake charmer calmly said, "No, Sahib, I can take care of this." He wrapped a pliable root around his upper arm as a tourniquet, reached into a small box, and took out a tiny black object which looked like a stone. He placed it on the finger where the fangs had entered, and then placed his hand on his knee. Soon he developed a severe tremor in the hand and began to sweat profusely. After five or ten minutes, the tremor quieted down and, finally, the black stone dropped off his finger. He picked up the stone, tapped it on his flute, causing several drops of viscid yellow fluid to flow onto and discolor the gourd flute.

My father asked what the black stone was and the snake charmer told him it was the brain of a Himalayan tree frog which had been slowly processed in heat so that it was carbonized. All the snake charmers in India used these to treat their bites. After approximately thirty such treatments, the accumulation of cobra venom in their system was apt to cause neurological damage and they would have to get out of the business. The snake charmer then took the black stone, placed it in his little box, and told us he would take it home and boil it in milk, with spices, before putting it away for future use.

This scene is the most vivid memory I have of the effect of energy and vibration as a healing tool.

I now believe the time has come when ancient concepts and healings can begin to be validated by modern research. Dr. Candace Pert in her book, <u>Molecules of Emotions</u>, gives some insights into what is taking place as these snake charmers heal themselves when she says that, " Mind doesn't dominate body, it becomes body; body and mind are one. I see the process of communication we have demonstrated; the flow throughout the whole organism, as evidence that the body is the actual outward manifestation in physical space of the mind." She goes on to say, "We know that the immune system, like the central nervous system, has memory and the capacity to learn. Thus, it could *be said that intelligence is located not only in the brain, but in cells that are distributed throughout the body. The traditional separation of mental processes, including emotions, from the body is no longer valid."*

It is rewarding to see ancient therapeutic tools, which we knew worked but did not understand, are now becoming understandable through modern technology and research, helping us understand why the carbonized brain of an amphibian ancestor of the cobra had the sort of energy that could vibrate with the venom of the cobra in such a manor as to draw it out of the body of the snake charmer.

Chapter 9
Imperfect Yet Growing

The strength of the work mentioned in the previous chapter comes from many sources. It is a work in progress on every level. As it grows, is taught and practiced, it becomes living medicine in the fullest sense of the words. Remembering that "God uses imperfect people to do His perfect work," is a useful means to help us reserve judgement as this work enjoys its successes and studies its failures. Resisting our natural tendencies to judge ourselves and those around us harshly as we find fault in areas where we expect perfection, will help us avoid useless misery. We really don't know what perfection is, anyway. Only God is good so we have no choice other than doing the best we know.

The ideals we develop during our lifetime bring us together and allow us to grow. Ideas, on the other hand, may give us comfort when we cling to them as fact, but they close both our minds and our hearts to that which new experiences can teach us. They separate us. We have to move out of that comfort zone in order to keep growing and developing our ideals. This vital growth is almost certainly uncomfortable, often filling us with a fear of the unknown, a fear of change that leaves us stuck in one place, paralyzed, not fully alive. Once we take that step towards an ideal we are able to face our fears one at a time, bringing our heart, soul and mind together. Taking that first step sets us free.

Last year I was given a bonsai tree that I dearly love. I know it will never grow any bigger than it is because I cannot take it out of the pot in which it is planted. Its roots cannot stretch out and get any bigger; its limbs will always be pruned back. It is a dwarf tree, and it will always be one. It has its place in my home, and is meant to be what it is. If, however, I want it to change and grow, then I must take it out of that pot. It has to embrace life and change if it wants to grow to its full size.

When we complain about someone or something making us uncomfortable, perhaps it is because we are being offered a chance to grow and we need to loosen up. If we turn away from the source of our discontent and restrict ourselves, we risk restricting our growth, and we may be stuck in the little container equivalent to first grade for the rest of our lives, simply because we are afraid to let go of comfort and make the move to second grade.

Comfort is, well, comfortable. It can provide us with needed rest and support, but maintenance of an old comfort zone takes a lot of energy and it effectively prevents many experiences that could enrich and enhance our lives. We cannot stay in the comfort of our mother's womb forever. When the time comes we must all go through the separation of birth in order to become a functioning, independent soul.

There may be times we have to give ourselves a bit of a kick in order to break away from that protective wall that is, in fact thwarting us. On occasion, life will do the kicking for us, and difficult circumstances or an illness will force our hand. Then we have to risk growth in order to survive.

I met a lady at a dinner party recently who had moved here from Cleveland. The conversation turned, as it often does, towards the weather in Arizona. There's a lot of sun, but at this time of the year it happened to be pleasantly warm. Most of us were enjoying this environment, but not this lady. Because of the weather, she hated Arizona, she hated the sunshine. The people were okay and her home life was fine, but she was miserable. She loved the cloudy, cold, even freezing, snowy weather of Cleveland. In Arizona there was nothing but sunshine, and more sunshine, every day. Someone asked her how long she had lived here in Arizona, to which she replied, "Fourteen long years."

I felt sorry for her. Instead of enjoying the beauty of her home, she was stuck in Cleveland. Instead of recognizing the love and light with which she was surrounded, she was miserably stuck in hate.

Life is wonderful; it is a privilege to be alive! The juices that flow within us are the re-creation of what surrounds us below and above. We are part of the Tree of Life and the wonder of the entire life cycle. If we can let go of the fears that paralyze us and walk through the forest of the trees of life, a confidence develops with each step, be it a little one or be it a huge leap. That "journey of a thousand miles," that "begins with a single step," does not mean that any one journey will be easy or make life perfect, but that each of us imperfect beings is capable of doing great work.

The head of a Hospice organization once told me, "When

we see one patient with cancer for instance, what we see is one patient with cancer. Notice, we do not call this person a cancer-patient." It struck me that the difference between a patient with cancer and a cancer-patient is huge. They are nowhere near the same, and when one sees and understands the difference, the approach with each patient becomes unique and more meaningful. It is specific to the individual patient, not a protocol fitting any patient working with cancer. It is not just a routine but is a flexible approach that considers the changes occurring in the patient's life.

In other words, the histology of each cancer may be the same as other cancer patients' histologies, but the cells of that particular person are uniquely their own. All the influences in a person's life force are unique to that individual and as long as a person is alive, their body is constantly changing. As these changes occur, treatment must also change in response to the patient.

I have a friend who is challenged with third stage colon cancer. She told me she was dismayed by a comment from a well-meaning friend. Trying to be caring but not knowing how to approach the subject she said, "Fortunately, the kind of cancer you have is one that still allows you the possibility of two to four years of life." My friend knows the cancer is not the central part of her life, and she responded, "I am not looking for two to four more years, I am looking to get my life back. There's so much I have to do. I want to be living my life to the fullest. The cancer cannot take over my life."

As I listened to her story I realized that her well-meaning

friend had been talking about colon cancer, that she had given the identity of colon cancer to her friend. She was not talking about my friend, the person. Meanwhile, my friend was saying," The person that I am does not accept that identity. My life is full and I have a disease."

The process of life, no matter what the duration, can be experienced fully.

Disease has no business making us forfeit the natural occurrences of our lives. When we take on what a person, a doctor, a piece of advertisement suggests we become distracted by the perceived outcome. And so we are chained to fear, becoming a disease, a problem to be fixed; we forget that our life is a process. We miss the opportunity to use the condition of our life to summon the courage needed to aim for our purpose. My friend honored her ideals, honored the life she was given; the malady that she has does not dictate who she is. She is a woman that has a disease.

His Holiness the Dalai Lama said, "Our prime purpose in this life is to help others. If you can't help them at least do not hurt them." In matters of health, I have found that working with the physician within, each patient I can listen to her own insights, which often hold the key to wellness. To achieve the results we desire we need to become responsible. Changes can be challenging.

It was during my journey to understand my medical problems that I found the physician within me, the one Dr. Gladys had told me about. The universe was generously on hand to help, but first the search for knowledge had to take place.

Angels disguised as Old Ladies, nurses, doctors and muses appeared to offer their guidance. The trick was to be willing to listen to them, and take their offerings to my physician within. The remedy I needed was change.

Dr. Gladys had given me a list of things to eat, as well as a list of things I was not to eat. She knew that I would have a hard time with the idea because I wanted magic pills, so she had already told me that how I handled my chronic challenge was a choice that was mine to make.

Life is a journey to be lived, not a problem to be solved. When we put our energy into and our attention on living our life fully, we get the chance to know ourselves for who we are. If, on the other hand, we allow the normal, natural parts of our lives to become a disease process, then we end up dealing with that disease, and we cease to know ourselves. The trick is to create the balance that allows us to have a disease without being the disease, still knowing who we are.

Now, years later, I make every effort to consume less sugar, or foods that convert to sugar. I do not eat wheat or things made with wheat. Now the brewery once in my gut no longer produces the alcohol that literally made me drunk. Change was not easy; sweets comfort me but I have learned to step away from a comfort that was not serving me, to accept the responsibility for my health.

Chapter 10
Gathering of The Eagles

Mothers will tackle any problem that troubles their children because they deeply care about them. Dr. Gladys carries this maternal response far beyond her immediate family; she is invested in the whole human family and she is dedicated to securing the best possible health for the largest number of people. Weaknesses in the system trigger in her a strong maternal reaction to correct them. No matter the condition, no matter the odds, she marshals all the resources she can find to correct the problem. Unfortunately, changes in the health care system come even less easily than changes in some people's eating habits *conscious effort and determination are the tools we need to bring changes to our health care system. I went to Washington, D.C. with a purpose to reform healthcare. Since January 2009, The Foundation For Living Medicine has called together two major conferences of people involved in the transformation of our national healthcare system. The meetings have been dubbed, "The Gathering of the Eagles" because, having observed eagles soaring, I know them to be calm, observant, focused, able to see clearly what is below because of their vision and height of flight. These gatherings have brought together a group of leading holistic physicians, nurses and integrative healthcare providers, all of whom have practiced for many years with a similar calm, careful focus, and clarity of vision. They have worked together to create a white paper filled with ideas and solutions that reflect these qualities and will continue their dialogue at the next conference in the spring of 2013. The vision they share is of a new health care model that would mitigate the current health care crisis and, over time, negate it by creating a blueprint for a new approach to healthcare that shifts some of the paradigms in medicine. These paradigm shifts will offer both tangible and intangible benefits and will reduce costs. The overarching recommendation is to promote a model change in healthcare that changes focus from treatment of disease, with heavy emphasis on pharmaceutical intervention, to treatment of people, stressing prevention and wellness through lifestyle change, patient/provider relationships and the integration of care.*

This represents a fundamental change of focus from fighting disease to the promotion of wellness in individuals, families and communities. In this model, the emphasis is on understanding and viewing health as the wholeness of life, not just the absence of disease. It promotes discontinuing the current war model in medicine of killing disease, eradicating virusses, and eliminating symptoms and concentrates on behaviors that promote health, wellness and wholeness, acknowledging the innate ability of the body to heal, as well as the importance of spirituality in that healing process. It further recognizes the significant benefits that result from the integration of alternative and complementary medicine into a national routine health care strategy.

Such a change in fundamental modes of medical care supports a transition from an archaic healthcare delivery model of competition and profit driven decisions, to one of collaboration, partnership and outcome effectiveness for all concerned. It further appreciates that medical research is on the frontier of new discoveries, using energy medicine and adult stem cells. Each modality having the potential to play a vital role in healthcare must be organic and equipped to implement new treatment options that are proven to be effective.

The McGarey Foundation's Gathering of the Eagles Task Force will work in concert with government agencies, educational institutions, and the healthcare industry to create relevant policies and to serve as an incubator for new integrative programs. Specific policy areas supporting this framework include:

Promotion of Wholeness, Infusion of Compassion into Healthcare, Recognition of Women as Important Healthcare Decision Makers, Support of Holistic Pregnancy and Childbirth, Funding of Research for Alternative and Complementary Modalities, Standardization of Certification and Licensure.

It takes passion, vision and wisdom to gather the energy that is needed to join the science of medicine with the practice of medicine; having practiced medicine for sixty-six years, Dr. Gladys has long wrestled with the need for the marriage of the science of medicine and the art of healing.

A surgeon can suture a laceration, but only the patient can heal the wound. Pharmecuticals need to be freed of their unrealistic roles as first choice therapies. Changes are upon us and the time has arrived for Living Medicine, a healthcare industry of human service in which the physician within the patient is empowered to participate in the healing process. Education and teamwork between patient and physician, coupled with a deeper understanding of the living process, is required; the time has come to recognize and utilize the innate ability of the body to heal, and healthcare providers need to come respectfully together with healthcare recipients, enlisting government and business in a joint effort to make a healthy life desirable and available to everyone.

Chapter 11
Two Shawls

There is something comforting about old trees: their branches are far reaching, they protect birds and insects, and they give us shade. Their roots hold on to the earth for the benefit of the lives, and Old Ladies do the same thing. Sadly, trees age as women do, and ultimately, regardless of where they were planted, they must sometimes come down.

Decades ago a friendship arose between the late Dr. Elisabeth Kübler-Ross, born in Zurich, Switzerland, and Dr. Gladys. Dr. Gladys helped souls make the transition into human bodies at the births she attended. Dr. Kübler-Ross helped ease the transition out of their bodies at the time of their death. Together they, with other like-minded physicians, helped to found the American Holistic Medical Association.

Dr. Kübler-Ross's groundbreaking book, <u>On Death and Dying</u>, changed the world's attitudes toward the inevitable end of every human's life. She was a psychiatrist and her findings on the subject are still used and discussed today under the name of the Kübler-Ross Model. In this model she recognizes five stages of grief. First there is denial, after that, anger, then bargaining, followed by depression, and finally, acceptance. She believed *that life should be lived half-working and half-dancing and I have enjoyed the years during which we shared our work and our lives.*

Elisabeth Kübler-Ross was a strong woman, and with her training, wisdom, and keen powers of observation she was a good judge of character. She recognized a quality in my sister Margaret, something that was pure and completely honest, with no need for pretense. My sister Margaret is a nurse; her work shines in a world of darkness. She didn't do the big things that Elisabeth did, but the little things that she has done day by day have created an enormous life. Elisabeth shared the characteristics she recognized in Margaret and she displayed her attributes with more force, but differences of intensity aside, they were both sisters to me in similarly supportive ways.

No matter how we define culture, family, relatives or friends, the connections we make above ground solidify the root system of humankind. The very roots of our individual beings have taken the same elements from the earth as have the roots of the beings around us. The soil gives up its substances, sometimes toxic substances that endanger the tree, but the roots absorb and filter, taking the brunt of the harm so that growth can continue. We all benefit as part of the same magnificent tree of humanity. We are all sisters; we are all sharing that from which the roots have grown, we all share similarly tangled roots and experiences, roots that have received nourishment from the same sources roots that filter, clear, and nurture us through life. We have put these roots down, in order to support a tree, some parts of which may be windblown, broken, withered and weak while others are very much alive, supple and flourishing. All parts remain because the roots are active, holding tightly to the soil that feeds them as they prevent erosion and landslides. Like older people, they are still there connecting, filtering, clearing, nurturing and supporting.

From 1926 until 1929, I was a student at the Woodstock School in the Himalaya Mountains. During this time there was no diagnosis of a condition called Dyslexia, though that was part of who I was. I had difficulties reading words and certainly with adding and subtracting numbers. I was considered the class dummy. As a result of a then nameless affliction, I was made to repeat the first grade, and school became a daily torture. At the end of each day I climbed 1000 feet up the mountains to our home. There, to my good fortune, my nanny (in India called an Ayah) sat on her haunches, wrapped in her rough woolen, drab green shawl, waiting for me. She knew I was a pretty sad little girl but I knew, sad on not, under this shawl I had a place of safety and healing. When I got close, Ayah held out her arms and said, "Ider Aw," "Come here." She would wrap her arms around me, and I would be covered by the shawl. There, in the sacred place under the shawl and the safety of her arms, I stayed for as long as I needed. That simple gesture gave me what I needed to face another day in school. It is important for us to each have a place of safety and healing, a protected sacred place where we can recuperate and be ready to meet the next life struggle. I have kept that rough homespun shawl all these years; it is one of my most treasured possessions.

Dr. Gladys climbed 1000 feet every day to find her place of safety. As we walk through our lives, we too find what we need. The answers we search for are never too far, and if we look for them we can find them. Although we each think our problems and struggles are uniquely ours, they occur in every household, every community, and every country. The Old Ladies of the world are aware of this and perhaps we should look for those protecting arms, withered and fragile though they may be.

India was torn apart in 1947. The conflict between Hindus and Muslims had erupted. My parents and my physician brother, Carl, were in India then, doing what they could with the tools available to them: inoculating against disease, patching up wounds, setting bones, treating malaria, helping with the birthing of babies, and handling cures or remedies for other maladies and even digging graves for those who had lost their lives in India's struggle.

Mahatma Gandhi was also there, giving his breath, energy and life to help his people come to an understanding of each other. He was working for the healing of his beloved country with the tools he had in much the same way that my parents worked with their tools to heal individuals.

A friendship and a great deal of respect developed between my parents and the Mahatma. He gave my mother a shawl made of blue Kashmiri wool. It is much different from the one my Ayah wore, but this shawl came to represent for me another safe place; the one that Mahatma Gandhi held in his heart for his people.

Love, caring and compassion are what these two shawls carry with them. One, the love of a simple illiterate woman for a troubled little girl; the other the love of a great man for the millions of people in his troubled country. They are both treasured possessions, and on very special occasions I wear the blue one, taking within me the healing energy of those who made it, those who wore it and the reason why it was given to my mother. When I wear the shawl my ayah gave to me, the feelings of safety envelop me no matter what the life struggle is. When children cling to their tattered blankies they know this feeling of finding a safe place in simple objects that carry great power in the love they manifest.

Perhaps the significance of these shawls led me to become a weaver. I have made some blankies for babies, and I find weaving fascinating. Although the machines that do the weaving have changed through the years, the ancient craft itself has not, and the finished product is still worn and used in thousands of ways.

Weaving by hand demands planning and commitment. From the fiber to the spinning wheel to the weaver's loom and its tools, weaving requires an investment of self.

Although it is very mechanical with its spindles, and shuttles, spools, it is rather like giving birth because a transformation takes place once the process itself begins.

Standing in front of a warping board, yarn at the ready, the very first time it took a moment to realize that my body was swaying from left to right as I began to string the yarn. With the movement of the yarn and my body, I began to feel a subtle shift: I was the weaver, I was the yarn, I was the process, and I was the prayer.

Now that I am an old pro at weaving, I know that when I weave, every movement is infused with much more than warping board, loom and yarn. There is a prayer interlacing the strands of life. The roots beneath the forest lead the way to something larger. We have sisters who are not family members and we receive safe harbor from whatever winds tear at us in the forest supported by our roots

PART 3
The Bark

While the tree is alive it must wear a cloak of protection, much like the shawls of which Dr. Gladys speaks. The bark of a tree provides its main defense. In much the same way, our clothing shields us, not only from the elements of nature, but from the elements of society. We use clothes to create the impression we present to the world. They provide us with a shelter in which we can grow change, improve, and fortify ourselves.

A tree's twisted roots, long curved branches, distinctive leaves, and sensually reproductive buds cannot bloom and continue the circle of life with new seeds and fruits without the necessary protection of the bark. Those of us who have had extended exposure owe our endurance to the layers of bark that have protected us, that have been there to hold our history and our juices together. We have grown and gotten tougher with age to protect something precious inside; under our bark we are able to hold the history of what went on at the root.

As humans we have opportunities for shelter beyond our obvious physical protections. We can find safety in a hug we receive when we are feeling low, comfort in a cat that purrs when we caress it, serenity in a star-studded sky that reminds of our inclusion in an incredibly vast power where there is a marriage of elements similar to our own circle of life.

Chapter 12
Be Gentle When You Touch Me

When I began to write this book with Dr. Gladys, I did not know that my pen and my heart would take me to so many unknown places. She has enriched my life with a bounty of new things to see and touch, and acceptance has become routine, and gentle observance has become second nature.

I touched the bark of a tree and felt its roughness. Although it was not a painful sensation, the intensity was unanticipated and I wanted to withdraw my hand, not touch the tree; it was unfamiliar and felt a little threatening. Perplexed, I began to examine what felt like fear in a situation that was clearly not dangerous. The exploratiion took me back to my childhood.

When I was young I was afraid of the dark. I could not explain why then any more than I could explain my reaction to the tree bark. The conclusion I have reached is surprisingly simple: the unknown or unanticipated is unsettling at best, terrifying at its worst, and the journey from fear of the unseen to acceptance of the unknown is as intimidating as it is liberating.

Dr. Gladys has suggested that such perception based fears might stem from a natural desire to will away our fears. No matter how desperate our desire to control a situation that is not to our liking, we will never have any control over the workings of the universe. We do have control over our own thoughts and actions, and that is what Dr. Gladys gently offered me in these three Hindustani phrases:

"Tauba, Tauba;" "Oh my! Oh my!"
"Khatman Ho Gaya;" " It is finished."
"Jo ho so ho;" "What will be will be."

I had never considered the possibility of philosophy with no particular word to convey desperation, one that only allowed for, "It is finished." Desperation will not take us from point A to point B, but the recognition that, "It is finished," certainly can. Once we stop fueling the thoughts, it is indeed, finished. We can start fresh, and the wheel of life continues its revolutions.

My perception of leprosy will serve as a good example. Initially leprosy, to me, was no more than word spoken about an unfamiliar and irrelevant condition. Having heard of Mother Teresa's work to heal the pain and suffering of lepers in Calcutta, the reality of the disease was not part of my reality and I could not relate to it. Living on the opposite side of the earth effectively removed it from the reach of my consciousness, or perhaps I am directly descended from ostriches. That changed when Dr. Gladys shared her experiences with me.

Dr. Gladys returns to touch the soil of the land of her birth as often as time, money and other demands permit. In 2004, to ensure that they were healthy and leprosy-free, she examined 900 children residing in the homes started by her family.

In India the fear of leprosy makes a leper untouchable. He must live his life apart from society, knowing that the very bark of his tree of life, his skin, is offensive to others. Although physical pain is not part of the disease, the pain of this dehumanization is real. A leper's children are the lowest of the low in India. No matter how bright or promising they are, they can never overcome this stigma once it is known that their parents were lepers.

This prejudice is offensive to me, but in all honesty I cannot claim to be free of similar weaknesses and, to be fair, I lacked sufficient information about the disease of leprosy without educating myself.

Mycobacterium Leprae, isolated in 1873, is the cause of leprosy. It is transmitted through prolonged intimate contact, through mucous membranes and open wounds. Although similar to AIDS, it is not a sexually transmitted disease. Neither are genetic factors the cause; it is not inherited and today it can be cured.

Still, those infected with leprosy are abandoned by the indifference of the world. Ignorance of scientific discoveries and advances has allowed the devastating prejudice against lepers to continue. Life has a way of preserving and presenting challenges that no longer, perhaps never did, exist. Humans are a strange lot, filled with fears we could overcome, many of which we know are unfounded. It is a difficult task for a people, a country, the world, to trust rather than fear change.

The secrets of our fears are often swept under a rug of our own making; when I was young the identification of my fear of the dark did not automatically bring on the light. It took me years to find the light switch. The resistance to the reality of leprosy is all the more understandable because, in truth, not all branches of the tree of life are able to grow to the light.

The World Needs Old Ladies

Chapter 13
The Physician Within You

In the ancient worlds of Greek mythology Hygieia, Goddess of Health and daughter of the God of Medicine, Asclepius, gave us our word "hygiene". When we clean our hands today, we are honoring this old medical goddess who thought that clean hands were a good idea. Of course today we have scientific proof of the value of clean hands because now we know about the bacteria our hands can transport from one place to the next.

Stem cells have been around for as long as we have but today we understand them better. They are the roots that make us what we are; human. Dr. Gladys got quite excited when she explained that in their undifferentiated form, these cells are what heal our body.

The Old Ladies of wisdom and medicine can trace their roots to the beginning of history. Women, the grandmothers and the mothers from Mesopotamia, Egypt, Greece, Rome, the mountains of India and China, and those of the Americas, have been passing the universal knowledge they have accumulated from one generation to the next since they first arrived here. They are the stems and they are the roots; they are the bark. They hold, filter, translate, protect and transport knowledge that they have gained from their experiences, often at great risk, always protecting the true nature of healing.

Since the beginning of time, the physician priest/priestess has known that true healing is more than curing a disease. The physician, as a priest/priestess, made contact with the spiritual nature of the patient and called upon the mystical nature of the person to bring about the healing. The physician-priest, the healer, the shaman, using what physical modalities their tradition had taught them, made this wisdom available at an understandable level and called on the innate healing power of the patient to do the healing.

Perhaps the ancients knew something about the spiritual nature of our beings, something we seem to have forgotten as we have become more knowledgeable about our physical nature. Although when our modern universities emerged, the patriarchal influences excluded their mothers and sisters from these institutions; the teaching of women by women never stopped. Even the most skeptical of modern physicians of today must sometimes face the fact that some patients get well when they have no business getting well while others, who seem to have everything in their favor, do not. Medical doctors, their patients, and their patients' families and many others live with this mystery every day.

I have been in the practice of medicine since 1946, perhaps longer than your life span. While I was in medical school penicillin was discovered and the atom bomb was exploded in Japan. The advances made in the field of medicine since those years are exciting, stretching our minds as it wages a war against disease.

It is an unfortunate reality, however, that the field of medicine has become a war machine; all its energy seems to be directed toward destruction and killing. We kill bacteria, eradicate AIDS, eliminate diabetes; we have even evolved a language that is against life itself. We talk about antibiotics, anticonvulsants, antihistamines and even anti-ageing. We create groups such as cancer support groups, epilepsy support groups, and so on, but by means of our focus our efforts end up addressing the diseases, not supporting the persons who have them.

As I became more aware of this, I saw that we, as physicians, had essentially forgotten the patient as we focused on the disease so that the disease had the patient, not that the patient had the disease. Even natural processes such as pregnancy and birthing had become diseases and we began working with the mother and the baby as if we were dealing with a disease, not the most natural process of life itself.

Somehow in our arrogance and our desire to be in control of all of life's processes we took away the individual patient's understanding that true healing was something that came from within. We forgot that ultimately each one of us, by necessity, does our own healing. Physicians and healthcare providers are there to help us with the healing process, but they do not do the healing; we do that ourselves.

When women were excluded from the universities, physicians proclaimed themselves on top, much like the ancient gods did. They clearly forgot that it was primarily the spiritual aspects of humanity with which shaman, healers, and priest physicians worked, in order to affect the physical world.

In my practice I have asked people to activate their personal power, the innate power to heal that each one of us has. As interdependent beings we can encourage and assist in the healing process, in ourselves and in each other, but no one can make another person get well. Each of us does have the power to reclaim and activate our life force individually and bring about a healing within our own being.

I have always known that there is something mystical and almost magical within each one of us. Love, compassion and understanding facilitate healing and it happens in unexpected ways. For many years I have termed this healing force within each of us "the physician within." I have been excited and encouraged as patients have activated the physician within themselves, sometimes against great odds, to bring about their own healing. I have seen, supported, and even coached the physician within my patients throughout their healing process because it is that physician within that brings about the healing.

A few years ago, I had a ruptured esophagus and it was the mysteries of healing cells that helped me heal. Doctors in the hospital advised my husband and me that my chances of survival were very slim, but they added that with the advances in medicine, there was a procedure that could be performed to save my life. The process they had in mind would permit me to receive fluids through a tube that would replace the damaged esophagus, probably for the rest of my life. I really wanted a different answer.

I had heard Dr. Gladys talk a great deal about the power of the inner physician that resides within each individual. Although not a doctor of medicine, I decided to access the physician that Dr. Gladys said was within me. I consider myself to be a spiritual person, and I believed that my spirit would have to get involved if I were to outlive this medical situation. I am not one who prays in a conventional sense, but I knew if I quieted my fear of dying, released my anxieties and trusted this physican inside that my fears would not control my outcome. I decided to allow forces I could not see or understand to take part in my recovery by accessing the physician within myself. Having made this decision, it took about seventeen days to see the improvements.

Today my food travels through the esophagus I was born with, and some medical people have called my cure a miracle. Many did not understand, though they could see from the battery of scans, X rays and MRIs that my esophagus had been healed of a serious tear.

I was fortunate to have been sufficiently exposed by Dr. Gladys to the idea that within me there was a healer and I am of the opinion that many of the ancient healers and many of the people who have experienced miracle healings have simply reached the place within from which healing originates.

My esophagus was repaired through my ability to gather the forces of healing within myself. I was able to activate and not abdicate. Today I am convinced that we all can do this, if we so choose. There are very good reasons to choose healing.

Through the years I have come to understand that "killing medicine" does not really heal people. It is the concept of living medicine, using therapeutic modalities that enhance and strengthen the life force within a patient that allows healing to take place. We are after all, living cells responding to energies, to music, to love, and to prayer. When we shift our focus to life and living, love and healing, true curative results take place and this modality is living medicine, which is life itself! It allows the life force to become the greater healer.

Therapies are enhanced by compassion. They are diminished by detatchment. A surgeon's skill can only be enriched when she listens to and involves the patient in the process of healing.

The physician within each one of us knows why we are sick and what we can do about it. Enhancement and strengthening is what the adult stem cells within our bodies are doing every moment of every day; they know where we are sick, and how to repair the damage that has been done. The research being done on adult stem cells supports what the ancients have always known; we heal ourselves. The potential of using our own body cells to repair our damaged body parts is the future of living medicine. When properly injected into the blood stream of a patient, these cells know exactly how to heal and where the healing needs to take place, but if a patient does receive an injection of the allogeneic adult stem cell and healing does take place within the tissues of the body, it then becomes more important that the person cherish this living body and keep it as healthy as possible. It becomes incumbent on each one of us to discover if anything in our lifestyle has caused the problem in the first place, and to do what we can to correct it.

Stem cells are the mystery, the magic, and the very soul of healing. Todays adult stem cell therapy is living medicine at its finest because we are using the essence of the life force itself to bring about healing at a depth that has not previously been available to us. Even the physicians who are not within us are able to access and harness the healing, living, loving parts of ourselves for our benefit.

This scientific advance in healing cannot deny its similarity to the mythological goddesses and healers of ancient time, who, for thousands of years, have known how to assist some force within their patient to develop the right environment to heal. Today when a mother lovingly kisses her little girl's boo boo, she activates the stem cells that bring about the healing and this is true healing. Were the goddesses and healers of old simply communicating with these forces of life themselves, the stem cells?

There is an old parable about God creating man and looking for a place to hide the soul so that it would not be abused. He looked in the heavens and the earth. He rejected the highest mountain and the deepest ocean, and even the deepest cave on earth, because man would find it there. And so it is that we find the soul within these living cells.

We have been given a window in time to reclaim our divine heritage, and to do the things, which will keep our bodies and our earth healthy and alive. How do we now protect and care for this precious Holy Grail of health? This divine, now scientific gift, must be loved, nurtured, cherished and protected. If we abuse it, we will lose it again.

Many of my women patients through the years have had trouble accepting, loving and caring for themselves. Too often women are taught to love and care for others; to set aside *the love and care of themselves because it is selfish and self centered. It is easier for everyone to deal with the problems and needs of other people than with their own, but in addition, many women have been taught that self-neglect is God's will, that self love, self concern is wrong. We accept the idea that love is without judgment, but we reserve unconditional love for others. We ourselves have to be worthy of our love for ourselves and, knowing our own faults better than anyone else, we find it all too easy to judge ourselves unlovable. Doing so can be a life threatening mistake for ourselves as well as those we love.*

There is a very unselfish reason why flight attendants always instruct passengers to put on their own oxygen masks before assisting anyone else. They don't tell you to help yourself and just forget about everyone else, but they have to remind us to start with ourselves because it is so difficult for most of us to receive rather than to give. If we are to find peace and love for this world, we must start with ourselves, and in many instances it is the healthiest choice.

Chapter 14
The Gift of Life

During the course of a life, we encounter people who seem to possess an energy that attracts what they need when they need it. More often, our needs seem to go unmet for decades. This irony has puzzled me for years, but there seems to be a churning circular current in life where we all mingle and toss about, sharing love and friendship, and dispensing wisdom. In this current the seeds of our lives are dispersed so new trees can grow, but those seeds germinate on their schedule, not ours, and sometimes they demand patience. Life spins and as we age we recall conversations we had, words we heard; precious memories bring to mind what was waiting for the right occasion to germinate. Life does bring us the gifts we need.

It is unfortunate that we often think everything needs to happen quickly. Afraid to be left behind, we are always in a hurry. Drinking our instant coffee, delivered through our car window by a mechanical arm we rarely recognize as human. In our rush, we forget patience; we forget the joys of savoring each moment. We need to slow down enough to appreciate the bread and wine of past communions; they can help us when we're in need.

We must not forget the exquisite feeling of grass under

our feet, even when there seems to be no time to take off our shoes and wiggle our toes. The place impatient for our arrival is only in our mind. Wrongly focused on a ticking clock, we think we are too busy to unwind and we rush through the business we think must take priority. We multi-task, taking great pride in our efficiency, but we lose track of our needs and the needs of our loved ones until one day, we look at our own skin, our children, spouse and notice that the bark of our tree of life shows signs of aging.

If we look at the field of our past experiences, we may see the seedlings of new understanding. If we can go back to re-examine events of the past we may find new healing. When words and gestures from the past come to mind, I find myself sharing old lessons with others. When I remember Dr. Gladys's first prescription of, "Rest," it opens me to other ideas of hers that have been watching the clock for their opportunity.

We innately know the sacred places our minds and souls need in order to replenish our vital source. Why do we neglect them? Is it fatigue or the distraction from the speed at which we live?

As an Old Lady told me about the sad realization that the idea of emotional and mental peace was foreign to her grandchildren, she asked me where her grandchildren could experience peace and healing The pace of today's living: television, movies, games, and other distractions that surround us - makes it easy to escapes from the reality of our feelings. In addition to our adrenalin rushes we have drugs to dull our pain and relieve our boredom. With no ready solutions for this woman whose grandchildren cannot hear anything she says anyway, I shared some of Dr. Gladys's ideas.

In individuals, in homes and countries, there seems to be a loss of sacred, peaceful places, but the location of such a place is not far. To get there requires only a pause, intention and patience. It is within our heart that we find peace and healing. It does take some effort to find this place we all carry with us no matter who we are and where we go, but the grandchildren can find these things in their own time.

By over taxing, over using and abusing our bodies, we put ourselves in a position to encounter many chronic ailments. The invention of the electric light, the digital age, and the computer have made us a global society and when the sun goes down, we no longer take its advice to sleep. We continue on because we can turn a light on, power our computer and surf the internet to other continents. We force our bark to grow tougher than it was meant to be, expecting more of one another while we turn a deaf ear to the language of our own body.

"REST," her prescription said.

There has always been time for each of us to pay attention to the gift of life we are given. It is a privilege to be alive, yet we take this gift for granted. A tree cannot function without nourishment. A tree knows when to rest and when to bloom, it does not bear fruit out of season. Nature knows these things and yet we continue to disconnect from our own natural world. We forget that we are a part of the forest and our fruits cannot find their sweetness without respecting the cycles of the moon and the sun.

We must respect our needs the way trees respect theirs, if we seek health.

"REST," she wrote on her prescription pad.

In this matter of discovering who we are, deep within us, and in the fold of the garments left by our families, are circumstances that form the person that we are, awaiting detection. Like the bark of our tree protecting what is deep within, we too protect what we have inside of us. The gifts of the world are available no matter what we use to hide them. This cloak of protection keeps us safe from harmful elements and hurtful circumstances, yet within the creases of the fabric of life, the distinct choices we make give us the tools to acquaint each of us with who we are.

The bark of the tree changes both with time and with demands for growth. We of the human family are not excluded from the same processes. It is in this transition from youth to age that our life expression and choices continuously shine light on the paths we all travel. Our purpose is to know ourselves, to be ourselves and yet be one with God. There will be times when we rebel and seem to lose sight of our guiding principles. The idea is to persist faithfully while accepting the things we cannot change.

When Dr. Gladys talks about not being able to see around the bend as the road turns, not knowing what the future holds, she points out the importance of having enough faith to follow the ideal dictated by the choices we have already made. When we are holding a flashlight in the dark, we can only see as far as the beam of light will allow us to see. It is faith that allows us to know we will get where we need to go.

The map we need is deep within us but it is a gift we sometimes take for granted. In the depth of our being we find the stuff we are made of; we simply forget that it is there as we busy ourselves establishing a way of life without awareness.

A teacher friend of mine tells about one of her most brilliant young students, who was a difficult child:

"We studied astronomy in my class, and he became fascinated by comets, stars and planets. He asked if it was all swirling about, colliding on occasion, getting warm at times, cold at other times. He needed to know if we were all part of this dance,' Are we part of the fairy dust? As I dance around the room, I am the music. I bow and swirl and the fairy dust is in each note. I know I am a dancer. Does that mean I am part of that fairy dust God made?"

When I heard this Older Woman tell the story I realized the fairy dust was also spinning with me. We are individuals, yet we are all the same "One". The thing that distinguishes us best is the way we dance with the fairy dust and its music. Since the cells in our bodies know their reasons for being, I choose to honor the life that they contain as an expression of God, and of fairy dust.

From <u>The Buddhist Dhammapada</u> one can read:

"All that we are is the result of what we have thought: it is founded on our thoughts, it is made up of our thoughts. If a man speaks or acts with a pure thought, happiness follows him, like a shadow that never leaves him. For hatred does not cease by hatred at any time: hatred ceases by love this is an old rule."

Like Old Ladies, old rules have value.

The World Needs Old Ladies

PART 4
The Branches

What would I do if I had no limbs?

Whether branches are connected to our bodies, to government or to the tree of life they are, through their reaching and growing, able to change the shape of things both seen and unseen. The patterns of the ancestors are retained in them and communicated as they were received from the roots. Branches feel damages, but are able to heal their wounds if pruned properly they allow us to see the skies of hope. They extend what is sacred into the world, allowing new generations to go forth and they are part of the stories the tree has to tell because both the strong and the delicate branches offer memories from the roots and trunk for those generations to draw from.

The World Needs Old Ladies

Chapter 15
The Rocking Chair

No matter that our beginnings are all small, we are born as valuable individuals. No matter that we are born as individuals, we all carry the roots of our ancestors. Our mothers and fathers not only partook in this miracle, they are responsible for it. They are part of our DNA; we are part of theirs. We are all part of a universal plan.

Unfortunately, the contributions of Old Ladies often go unappreciated as do the gifts their age brings to future generations. Old Ladies have watched us grow and have much to teach us once we learn to listen. The gifts of women to women are indeed part of the underground movement Dr. Gladys talks about. It is the essence of the root system that holds the world together. Old Ladies, prepare the soil with their deeds in order to preserve their knowledge for daughters and granddaughters and they do it best when it is presented palatably.

Aside from being a doctor of medicine, my mother was also a seamstress. She no longer made dainty blouses to sell but she made most of our clothes. Her hand-wheeled sewing machine was fast and her hands were dexterous. I was about eight years old and had been invited to a birthday party She deftly made me a pretty dress with a ruffled skirt for this party. I loved it and I got dressed early for the party because I couldn't wait to put it on.

It was not quite time to go so I went outside to play. Our home was surrounded by trees and I could not resist the call of their majestic branches, so I climbed the tree, snagging the dress, and tearing the ruffles. Upset and dismayed, thinking that the dress with its torn ruffle was ruined, I stood guiltily below the tree, ruffles hanging and tears falling. I was afraid of the unknown consequences ahead and the probable destruction of my party plans. Mother looked at me, went inside, got some safety pins and pinned up the ruffles saying, "Okay, now you can go."

I went to the birthday party with the ruffles pinned up. Not having thought about the time and effort she had spent on that dress when I climbed the tree, it only took me a few minutes to ruin her handy-work. I knew it was my fault that my dress had been torn and that I had to attend the party with pinned up ruffles, it filled me with remorse. Mother understood my regret and felt no need for further punishment. The incident was over for me because of my age. It was over for my mother as well. Because of her wisdom she released the incident with her last pin.

As we go through life we remember stories and we remember feelings more clearly than we remember dates and times. The emotions we have are what follow us through the seasons of our lives. It is the remembrance of the incidents and the small events that have meaning, that mold the people we become.

We may not notice the bird that lands on the branch of a tree until we see the evidential nest. Awareness of such a manifestation of life can transform us with the realization of our inclusion in the simple wonder of baby birds in a nest.

Tree branches bend and sway in the breeze. How do little birds keep from falling out? How do they survive the rhythm of movement, the back and forth of life?

Thinking of my babies, pondering memories of rocking chairs, porch swings and rocking with my babies in my arms, I begin to wonder why this is such an integral part of our life as human beings on this planet. I remember my mother's rocking chair, and how it traveled with us, into the jungles of north India; how important it was when I was small to climb into her arms in that rocking chair. I remember how crucial it was for me as a mother to have a rocking chair where I could hold my babies and my older children as well.

I have observed many groups of women who have had children. When a young mother comes into the circle with a new baby, all the women who have had babies find themselves rocking in a matter of moments. It is instinctive, and although not all societies have rocking chairs or porch swings, all societies have women who rock their young. The understanding that the rocking movement is beneficial is intuitive.

My ayah did not use a rocking chair when I was a small child; when I would go to her with a problem she held me, rocking back and forth on her heels as she squatted on the ground. She didn't need to say anything; we just needed to rock. I remember her rocking me back and forth but I always thought it was to put me to sleep when I was being too rambunctious. These memories continue to bring me a smile.

My mother had a special place in her heart for the old

rocking chair that her mother used and when she rocked me she would tell me stories from her childhood. Perhaps the rocking had something to do with it but, without fail, within minutes of rocking me, she would fall asleep. Everyone knew she was not relaxed because of my hypnotic powers; it must have been the rocking. I promptly wiggled out of her lap then, in pursuit of my next adventure.

Wonderfully, our souls have known intuitively from the dawn of time that the rocking motion heals. We move our individual magnetic fields in relationship to that of the earth. The human body responds to the magnetic pull of the moon. We are largely made of water, and a response and resonance to the movement of the water within the structure of our individual cells causes tides in our bodies. The stimulation of rocking, which is constant and rhythmic, connects us to our innermost being.

Humans feel the pull of gravity that is within the planet even if we may be unaware of it. It is important for us to respond and restore the rhythm of our vibrations. The word for this is attunement. When we separate the syllables of this word, we find the words "at onement". It is this at onement that allows a closer vibratory relationship between what is within and what is without. Thought cannot accomplish this closeness; being attuned requires movement that facilitates our alignment to the world. Rocking does that for us.

The older a lady I become, the more I realize that the plants around me, along with my own body, are teachers, always ready for the next lesson. I have taken so much for granted. Even my loom has been teaching me, from within and without, about the value of movement. It is not surprising, then, that I feel I am the loom, the yarn, and the prayer.

Our bodies have a great deal to teach us. Resting can make listening easier. Our bodies, minds and souls need attunement and as we age, we require it even more. Perhaps nursing homes should consider equipping themselves with plenty of rocking chairs. Visualize a world in which people take five to twenty minutes a day to rock. We would be closer to both planetary and global at-onement.

The World Needs Old Ladies

Chapter 16
The Lifegiving Power of Humor

As Old Ladies reflect on their past, they are able to draw from the deep waters of their lives much that might be of use to the following generation. These waters carry a wealth of resources to help us achieve our goals, and one such resource is humor. Often humor allows people of age to guide us in the direction of the water's run.

Shortly before my mother died, she and my father were sitting out in my front yard enjoying the flowers. "John," she said, " look at that one plant. It is so full of blossoms, there must be four hundred blossoms on that plant."

My dad said, "Ach, Beth, there can't be more than forty." To that she said, "Just another zero, just another nothing; it's the same thing."

Little nothings are the ingredients that make our lives precious. Sometimes we complicate our lives by making something out of nothing. We can get through many things in our lives by not nurturing the little affronts or issues that grow larger if we focus on them and give them energy. We always have a choice to take offence or to let go of the many things that are said and done to us in life, and we must not take the elegance of our nature for granted. Old Ladies and their teachings embody this elegance and we must not neglect them. They can help remedy many of our problems and we can learn from them to plant our feet deep in the soil, find our roots, and grow strong.

The year was 1968; I drove my mother and dad to Kansas from Arizona. We were going to meet my sister-in-law so she could take them the rest of the way to Baltimore where they would spend the summer with her and my brother. At that time my mother's osteoporosis was severe and any movement caused deep pain. I had arranged the back seat with pillows so she would be as comfortable as possible during the long ride. I was very anxious and I drove faster than necessary.

Driving with my foot heavily on the gas through Globe and Miami, small mountain towns in Arizona, I heard a siren and soon there was a police car behind me. As I started to pull over Mother asked, "What happened?"

"Well, I was going too fast and the policeman is making me stop.

" Mother, in her sweet voice said, "I'll fix it." Without answering or paying much attention to her words, I pulled over and rolled the window down. As the policeman started to speak we heard a moan, and then a sharp cry from the back seat. Then we heard a deeper moan. The policeman looked concerned and asked if she was sick.

"Yes, she is very sick and I'm trying to get us to Kansas as fast as I can." "Well...," Another moan or two came from the back seat. "Okay, I won't give you a ticket, but please don't drive so fast."

"Yes, Sir," I said, as I rolled the window up and *pulled out onto the highway. My dad looked back at my Mother. "Oh, Beth, that was bad." "No it wasn't. I was hurting and I just let him know it." We made it to Kansas without any other problems.*

This is a wonderful example of the wisdom of respect mixing with the wisdom of a little disrespectful humor to achieve a positive outcome. Both generations of feminine energy made wise contributions, diametrically opposite though they were. The circle of family had a daughter stopping a car in accordance with the policeman's wishes, and the law, and a mother not about to let her daughter get a citation while giving help to her mother. Old ladies and their daughters have these unspoken conversations, and illness cannot stop a mother from protecting her children. *Although Gladys's mother could not control the movement of life, in a difficult circumstance she was able to enlist a bit of humor to bring new meaning to comic relief.*

The World Needs Old Ladies

Chapter 17
Aging Into Health

There is beauty in the aging process. Neglect and abuse are not part of it; it's a natural process and we can age into health if we are able to direct our energy and attention toward maintaining, perhaps reclaiming that health. It is tempting to try to cheat the progression of time, but in matters of nature it is best to practice the art of acceptance. Healthy practices help us to grow into the natural beauty of Old Ladies. As our bodies change, our hair and skin may require more effort than they did in our youth and there is no harm in seeking and using products that can help keep them healthy, smooth and beautiful. That said, we are also entitled to claim our own gained wisdom without fear of looking old, entitled to claim the power with which age has gifted us even when it is manifested as wrinkles. Our branches strengthen with every passing year; our leaves continue to renew, our stories continue to blossom, our fruits are still harvestable, and the seeds of our wisdom still hold rebirth. As we support growth and change in the life we have brought forth we must not neglect to celebrate our own growth and change.

Most wines improve with age, but every year on November 14 the French savor a certain new red wine, one that demands to be consumed as quickly as possible. Only for a passing moment can we relish the desirable quality of Beaujolais. The young wines of November 14, exceptionally, are not put on shelf to gather the bouquet of age; they are not meant to grow old, they are the memories of an afternoon. Only Beaujolais demands eternal youth by refusing to age; other wines welcome the changes time brings.

Our own life needs some preservation if we are to age into health. We don't need to be put on a shelf to become our best, but neither do we need to fear the loss of our youth by refusing to embrace change. If we can embrace aging it can reward us with knowledge and wisdom.

Most nations celebrate their birth proudly with every passing year. We should emulate them. We read the classics because they contain words and thoughts worth revisiting. We must not fail to respect the fact that we ourselves are anchors for acquired knowledge. We should celebrate our passing years and resist any denial by our culture of our contributions.

Not all cultures inundate their populations with advertisements promising to remove the essence of what has made each of us uniquely who we are. Many cultures value what we might consider eccentricity and many define themselves by their age. In China the elderly are a treasure. The Chinese language itself seems disinterested in defining the passage of time: they have no past tense so it is impossible to relegate anything to the past in China. Whether something is happening now, or whether something happened years ago, if it happened, it counts. Chinese culture reveres old women for their poetic wisdom and their appreciation of the present moment.

Western culture has a narrower view of worth. In our naïve pursuit of perfection we are encouraged to devalue anything that isn't current. We value new cars, new clothes, new styles. Trends make more money for businessmen than recycling does, so we are indoctrinated by the ad industry with promises to keep us fresh and up to date. Without help we aren't new enough even when we're young. What hope do we have if we're old?

Medicine and the best surgeons can only patch so much. At some point we have to make peace with the fact that our bodies can no longer sustain their former workload. They know they are no longer young no matter how we try to deny it. If we can accept that we have always been more than our physical bodies, it becomes easier to accept their decline.

Even when we are no longer able to do what we thought we came here to do, what we would call our life's work, life still needs to be lived, work needs to be done. This work that Old Ladies choose to do is every bit as important as the work they have already completed. It is work that supports humanity for the long haul. These Old Ladies are the roots that support the bark and the branches, the life force that begins at birth and has lived many seasons within each woman. This force deserves to be appreciated.

As women we do seem to have difficulty knowing our own value. We hesitate to do the things we were meant to do for fear of being misunderstood. We can choose to not let this fear stop our growth.

Alyce and Elmer Green were doctors in the late 1950's

who started the biofeedback movement in the U.S. Unfortunately, the Greens could not manipulate or control life's movement and Alyce came to suffer the ravages of Alzheimer's disease. Ultimately my friend Alyce no longer remembered me, but she remembered the feeling of love she had for me. The last time I saw her she said, "I don't know who you are but I know I love you." The living, loving, part of her being was still very much alive and she touched my heart. She was still worth something; she still had value. With the little things each old woman does, she brings a little something that is needed. This is why the world needs the Old Lady.

As Old Ladies remember their lives and the lives of those around them, they are able to draw from the deep waters of life what the next generation will need. The rise and fall of these waters carry with them the resources that support our potential. Many things that Dr. Gladys has said to me have helped me to grow into my own understanding of health. My aging is easer with the knowledge that I am part of an integral network holding humanity together. As long as I am breathing I am part of something larger than myself. With every breath I take in life, and I need to make no conscious effort to achieve this; it happens even when I'm sleeping. When I do become aware of my breath, I find that soon I can use it to clear my mind and become more peaceful.

When I was assisting mothers with the birthing of their babies, I saw that breathing with the contractions was essential. In natural birthing, which I always encourage if there are no factors indicating a need for medical intervention, the soon to become mothers learn early to take control of their body and their mind, one breath at a time.

Breathing must be coordinated and in tune with all of their actions. The baby was delivered oxygen through her mother during pregnancy and during labor this oxygen is crucial. This consciousness of the breath to life enhances labor and birthing.

In my practice of medicine, many of my patients who were suffering from various illnesses, including depression and fatigue, were often unaware of their breathing. They hardly breathed at all, using only the upper part of the lungs to make the exchange of air; they barely took in enough air to allow them to survive. It was definitely not sufficient to promote good health. At times as I listened to their chest, very often the breath sounds did not extend below the shoulder blades; exchange of oxygen in only the upper part of the lungs does not promote good oxygen-carbon dioxide exchange. I often discussed breathing with these patients. Once they became more aware of what it felt like to get a breath deep into the lungs and rid the lungs of accumulated residues, they began to feel better and their health improved.

Controlled breathing is not only a great stress reducer, but it allows oxygen to get to the brain and nervous system as well as to the muscular system, greatly reducing muscle spasms and tension.

The suggestion is to consciously, several times a day for short periods of time, breathe in joy and breathe out fear, breathe in energy and breathe out fatigue, breathe in laughter and breathe out anger. Be conscious of taking in the qualities of spirit that are desired as you breathe in regularly. Breathe out the qualities that represent negative aspects of being. I know of no disease process, whether it is physical, mental or spiritual, that is not helped on its healing path by conscious breathing.

Patience, persistence, and consistency are qualities we aspire to develop as we work towards healing of body, mind and spirit.

Looking at the words above I get irritated. I have never had the time to be patient; and since I have not had the time for patience, I certainly have not had any reason to be persistent. At least I can be consistent with my exasperation.

I have heard Dr. Gladys say something about impatience being a probable cause of stress and strain. She has talked about impatience and what it does to us. If nothing else, impatience causes us to age faster. It can also distress our digestive system. I felt I was young and vibrant when I heard her talk about this simple condition. I did have indigestion more often than not. I, however, did not feel stressed.

Often we do not have the patience to examine ourselves deeply; I know I am not alone in this. Sooner or later, however, there comes a time when patience is forced upon us as a necessity. Mine was tested when my oldest daughter began writing my biography, <u>Born to Heal.</u> *We were both impatient, yet knew we needed to be persistent to continue the work we had begun. Once the work was finished, we had to exercise patience again because we had released the manuscript to be published and between the loose pages of a manuscript and a book, there is yet another process demanding patience. The simple demand for patience and persistence involved in publishing a book was a lesson for both of us.*

The lesson of patience is deeper yet when healing is involved. By our very nature we are impatient people. We want to grow up too fast, until we are older and then we become impatient with the aging process and want to be younger.

Dr. Gladys and her notes! She could have been writing them just for me. Yet I know I am not the only one suffering the stress and strain of impatience.

True healing means making changes at the physical level, in the cellular and molecular structure of our being. If we try to bypass or speed up the process at any level, it is like trying to speed up a pregnancy, not allowing the baby to grow at its own rate. A premature baby can face a lifetime trying to rebuild what she missed in the natural growing process.

The quality of persistence goes hand in hand with patience. Our heart must persist in keeping the rhythm of its beat. If it tries to skip a beat or change its rhythm, our body is thrown into distress. It is wise to be persistent as we travel the path of life we have chosen according to our Ideal. This includes good health habits. Our bodies understand the rhythm of life. Without consistency, we fall short. When we work with our children, if we say one thing but live differently, we bring confusion into their lives and we confuse ourselves. We need to Walk Our Talk.

If we can begin to understand that life is a process and everything we do is part of that process, we can accept the ongoing reality of this life progression. When we do this we begin to relax and enjoy life as it is, rather than what we want it to be.

Patience and joy go hand in hand. It is hard to be impatient when you are laughing.

Like planting a seed, we must water it, consistently and persistently, waiting in patience to allow the tree of life to grow.

Chapter 18
Who Am I?

Old Ladies know how to open the doors of our subconscious by drawing upon their experiences to teach us. They make selections from the daily news, touch them gently and find personal applications that teach acceptance, integrity, and perseverance. They see absurdities, but they also see when people are beginning to outgrow the absurd and are ready to make a change.

While she was working in Afganistan Dr. Gladys met many women. Her work there was for and about women, and she touched many lives. Working with Shukria Hassan MD, the two of them gained an understanding of the conditions that the women of Afghanistan were facing and spent long and difficult hours trying to improve their situation without endangering them.

On a cool April afternoon after I returned home from Afghanistan, I had to go to the grocery store. I pulled on the red Afghani coat that had come home with me and went to the post office on my way to the grocery. As I left the post office and walked toward my car I passed a woman who said she liked my outfit. I didn't consider what I had on as "an outfit"; I was wearing the coat because it was cold. As I started my car she came toward it and stood by my window. When I rolled the window down she said, "I am so glad you have the courage to wear that. I often think I would like to wear something different but I'm afraid that people would find me strange, so I don't."

I told her that I thought we needed to express who we are. After thanking me, she walked to her car, wearing her gray sweats and I realized that our clothing choices do reveal some of who we are and what we have experienced. Whether we like it or not, this is what the world sees.

I was born in India in 1920. My parents were U.S. ctizens, but proving my citizenship is always a problem. My birth certificate is an old copy of a copy that has the seal of the US consul, but because it is a copy, it is not impressed with a seal. I have all my old passports and other documentation, but I remain officially suspicious.

In 1955, it took six months for me to get my medical license in Arizona. The absurdity was that I had already been in practice and properly licensed in Ohio for ten years. It all happened because my mother could not mail my original birth certificate for fear of its getting lost. It took endless effort and relentless persistence, but the licensing board finally accepted the stamped copy of my birth document. I only wanted to continue my practice of medicine.

I cannot help but think of a time many years ago, when I was a designer about to undertake the refurbishing of a hotel in a small town in the southeast U.S. The owner of this establishment noticed that my speech was accented and, consequently, he had a battery of questions: where were you born, what kind of an accent is it that you have, why are you wearing a suit, and where did you go to school? Somehow, based on my answers, he decided I was anti-American, and he wanted nothing to do with me. He went on and on, concluding, as I was gathering my design boards and other equipment, with the proclamation that I was a dangerous woman.

Armed with the answers I had given to his question, he even went so far as to telephone my employers to complain that they had sent him a French Communist from New York.

I graciously and wordlessly left the interview, puzzled by possible motivations for his reaction to me. Was he just afraid of things and people that had not originated in the world he knew? Were his perceptions the result of circumstances in which he was raised and educated? How did he come to the conclusions he reached about me? Ultimately I realized that the resolution of the problem was not mine to discover and I was able to let him go.

As we encounter difficulties in our lives it is important to remember that as a part of a large system of trees of life, the branches of our resources are many. The shelter and support they offer is capable of supplying any new growth that we might need in order to honor our individuality, as well as our connectedness.

The scenery around me as I walked to my car was green with life and birds escorted me with their songs. Mindful attention to the events presently at hand and a moment of acceptance made the drive to my office pure magic. Entering the freeway, I remembered the advice of an Old Lady who once reminded me of who I was, telling me to stay clear and honor my truth at all times. When she said it, I was puzzled, but here decades later, her words came back to me and the seed she planted had sprouted.

Chapter 19
Healthy Emotions

Life is a series of transformations, and like trees we must grow and change in order to thrive. In a natural environment a tree finds its boundaries the hard way; in an orchard or garden our assistance relieves it of certain natural consequences. By monitoring the speed and direction of its growth and grooming its branches we help it remain stable and strong.

There came a time in my life when surgery was the only solution for the serious condition in which I found myself. I was utterly paralyzed with fear of the unknowable changes that lay ahead, and found myself unable to act. Dr. Gladys shined a light for me with one of her stories.

I had a patient who was very sick; he needed surgery in order to live but he was paralyzed by his fear of it and was unable to agree to it have.

He was getting sicker by the day, but I could not reach trough his fears. He would avoid facing the truth of his situation by changing every surgical conversation to one of family and friends. He had been born with all his parts he clung to his irrational conclusion that he should go out with them. It was a way to disguise his fear and I understood that.

Finally, I asked him if he had ever done any work with trees. He said he was a gardener and loved trees. I asked him if he had ever had to prune a tree and he said, "Yes, of course." I asked why he did that and his immediate response was, "To keep it in better shape. Once pruned, it will be strong enough to grow plenty of new healthy branches to shade the area of the yard where it grows. By pruning it, I know the tree will not die, but will thrive for many more years, with a new look, and will support all around it".

He understood, as he talked about pruning, that he was talking about himself, and he could finally see that his surgery would serve the same purpose for him that pruning did for the tree. Removing that which no longer served him well would allow him to become stronger and healthier. He lived for many years after, although he was missing one kidney.

Such stories can free us from our unfounded fears. This one freed me. I had my back surgery, and now can walk, dance, and bend like a willow. I like to visualize the rods holding my back together as stalks of living bamboo. Life, like a coin, has more than one side; when we flip our fears, we open ourselves to the possibility of many joyous moments. Pruning the tree of life allows us new opportunities for growth.

During the first Gulf War, I had many patients who said they were depressed. As we talked I realized they were not depressed, they were grieving. They had family members or friends in the service, and they were sad. The world was wounded, and she was sad. I began to wonder about two words: grief and depression, since we were using them interchangeably. I decided to look them up in the dictionary and I found that grief and depression are not synonymous. Synonyms for grief revolve around suffering: sorrow, regrets, disappointment and distress. Depression's synonyms were rejection, gloom, feeling downcast. These two words have distinctly different definitions and our cultural blurring of these distinctions impairs our ability to deal with either of them effectively.

Once the differences were clear to me, the patients and I began to express and deal with symptoms from a deeper level of understanding. They realized they were not depressed, but grieving as their feelings of sadness shifted. Grief is an emotion we must all deal with at some point in our lives. It is an ongoing emotional process that each of us must handle in our own way because the situations that cause grief can be very different from person to person. Grief, unlike depression, cannot be medicated; it must be experienced. Only as we recognize our personal griefs, and allow ourselves to experience them, can we open ourselves to healing growth. Suppression of grief can become a deep-seated problem and it can result in physical symptoms.

Anger is another emotion that benefits from clear thinking. For good reason, none of us gets through life without experiencing some anger. We can use all the help we can get.

According to Aristotle:

"Anybody can become angry, that is easy, but to be angry with the right person, and to the right degree, and at the right time, and for the right purpose, and in the right way, that is not within everybody's power; and it is not easy.

Also Aristotle: "I have learned that anger is not incurable, if one wants to cure it."

Buddha said that a person is not punished for his anger, he is punished by his anger. In reality, anger is a neutral emotion, neither good nor bad. It is a natural part of our emotional makeup. There are times when anger helps a person heal; it can move them out of apathy. Anger suppressed causes many physical problems; and anger gone blind is hate. Our challenge is to learn and choose healthy ways to resolve the issues that have caused our anger.

Fear is never confused with other emotions. It is such a powerful emotion that it can immobilize a whole nation and, if we let it control us, it can completely stop our own growth. Ironically, fear can also spur us on to further growth. Each of us must find our own way of dealing with or making use of our fears, but only facing our fears and moving through them allows us freedom to move on.

Personally, I have found that when I am faced with a decision and I realize that I am making that decision on the basis of fear, it is probably the wrong decision. It's a signal to take another look at the problem, to look for an approach which is not driven by fear. Once I can make a conscious choice without fear, I feel more confident to act on it.

A patient of mine who had been a longtime smoker developed lung cancer. Having received all of the conventional therapy she one day called me and said, "They tell me my blood count is so low I need a blood transfusion. I don't want it." I asked her why and she told me that she was afraid of AIDS and hepatitis. This, of course, was a weak rationale in view of her impending death from lung cancer, but when '"FearSteps In Reason Steps Out.'" None of the reasons I could give her helped until I asked her to consider a new perspective. "Maybe there is someone in this world that loves you enough to give her life-blood for you. It is a life-giving act, and Jesus did say, "Perfect love casts out all fear." When she was able to take her focus off of fear and put it onto love, she was able to get the transfusion.

As humans we are blessed with emotions, many of which help to lighten our lives and ease our troubles. One such emotion is joy and our ability to experience it increases with study and cultivation. Joy can be learned. Joy can be earned.

The Indian poet Tagore has shared his experience of joy: "I slept and dreamt that life was joy. I awoke and saw that life was service. I acted and behold, service was joy."

My parents named me Gladys. I am glad about that because this name serves me well. My car license plate is a reminder to me, and to the people following me in traffic, it says, "BEGLAD."

Being joyous does not mean we will be exempt from difficult experiences. Life is full of mountaintops and valleys and as we go through the valleys we need a way to access the feelings we enjoyed on the mountain tops. Their perspective can often help us avoid getting stuck. Perhaps we need to recall the valleys, too, in order to appreciate the richness of contrast when we are basking on the mountaintops. Monotony is numbing and it stifles growth. Joy and sorrow need each other and either one of them is capable of moving us to tears. The most deeply joyful of us are those who have suffered great physical, mental or emotional pain. They have allowed themselves to experience difficulties without inhibiting them and they understand that such dark times harbor many positive potentialities. Brilliant autumn colors are made more vibrant by the black limbs and the trunks of leafless trees.

Joy comes from being present in the moment-by- moment experiences of life. True joy is not found in the superficial pleasures that joy is an attractive diversion, but is destined to end. Sustainable joy comes from a deeper place and it can ride right along with us through the valleys. Our challenge is to cultivate the joyfulness that will sustain us when we experience difficulty; the joyfulness that does not lose out to sadness. This joy does not depend on outside conditions, it is something that comes from the inner experiences of the at-one-ment of body, mind and spirit. We can be people who have had sad times without surrendering our joy. If our energy does get stuck at the level of the adrenal because of anger, judgment, disappointment, or fear, this at-one-ment is what gives us access to the smile or the laughter that can move the block.

Hope is a gift of strength to be reckoned with. Rabidranath Tagore calls it, "the bird who sings before the dawn."

I have watched as a patient, given up by her physician and expecting either to die or spend the rest of her life with disease or disability, respond to the smallest ray of hope with improvement. I have also seen recovery screech to a halt when hope dims.

When I was in medical school I was told never to give a patient false hope. In the actual practice of medicine, I soon learned that this was wrong and I don't believe there is such a thing as false hope. There can be false expectations and false information, but not false hope. Hope is one of the fruits of the spirit, and it can never be false. There are times when it is the only thing that pulls a person through difficulty. It is one of the most important tools any health giver has to offer a patient or a friend.

We cannot examine hope without examining faith and love.

Faith is spiritual, while belief is a mental attribute. If we have faith in the power of life itself, we can accomplish amazing things because our body responds to the strength of that spiritual power.

Faith is the very substance of the Tree of Life. It is the acceptance of the power of life itself. Its expression is personal, part of each person's uniqueness and since it does not really depend on the mental attribute of belief, it may or may not be part of a particular religious belief system.

Love is at the heart of life and healing. Love is the great connecter. When fear and anger separate people it is love and forgiveness that brings them back together. The Bible says "God is Love." Our experience of love on this human dimension, is the closest we can come to experiencing the presence of the Divine and our experience of love is a personal emotion. We can, and do try to describe it in words, but until we have recognized the experience of it we do not know it. In reality, we are all surrounded by love because we are alive. We become conscious of it when our hearts open to it. To be lovable we need to be love able. When we open our hearts to love it fills us and overflows to all of life around us. It truly is the essence of life itself. And it heals.

The World Needs Old Ladies

PART 5
The Leaves

Our Tree of Life could not survive without leaves. By transforming the sun's energy and allowing it to flow through the entire tree, leaves assure the future of the forest. No matter how large or small they are, leaves distribute the energy of the sun that is needed for survival. Before the sensual blooms can flower each spring, before the seeds of the future can set, the leaves must bud.

Humans need leaves, too, providing us with shade and shelter; they make the sun's energy useable while they keep it from burning us. Old Ladies and leaves have these commonalities.

From a distance we see a multitude of leaves on a tree. A close examination reveals the individuality of each leaf. Old Ladies are also individuals, each with stories to tell from her own tree of life.

The World Needs Old Ladies

Chapter 20
The Importance of Touch

Talking to an indigenous American grandmother, I first began to understand the universal value of hugging. She was talking about the leaves of a cottonwood tree on my property and she said, "Did you ever notice, every time the wind blows, even just a little, the leaves embrace the whole tree? It feels like the way babies hug their mothers." Her perception of the tree was different from mine and she didn't say much more about it, but those few words of hers return to hug me like the wind in that tree of mine.

Dr. Gladys hugs like that, and when she can't be physically present to give a hug, she puts one in a note. Sometimes she, too, reminds me of my cottonwood tree.

Hugging is a miracle medicine that can relieve many physical and emotional problems. It can help you to live longer, protect you against illness, cure depression and stress, strengthen family relationships and it can even help you sleep without pills. In lifting depression a hug enables the body's immune system to renew itself. It breathes fresh life into a tired body, and makes you feel younger, more vibrant.

I remember the first time I went to Dr. Gladys as a patient;

when the nurse took me down the hallway toward her office the doctor came out and gave me a hug. I nearly fainted because it was a first for me, but once I got over the shock, I found that I was feeling better already.

In my experience a hug will frequently not only help to relax a patient, but will actually start the therapeutic process.

WHY GOD MADE HUGS

"God saw that we would need to know a way to let these feelings show. So God made hugs a special sign, a symbol of a Love Divine. A circle of our open arms holds in love, and keeps out harm. One simple hug can do its part to warm and cheer another heart. A hug is a bit of heaven above, that signifies God's Perfect Love". Author Unknown

Hemoglobin is the part of the blood that carries vital supplies of oxygen to all organs of the body, including the heart and brain. An increase in hemoglobin tones up the whole body, helps prevent disease, and speeds recovery from illness. Researchers have discovered that when a person is touched, the amount of hemoglobin in their blood increases significantly.

I have a story of a grandfather whose daughter gave birth to a very premature baby. She weighed only a pound and a quarter and the baby had to be placed in an incubator. The infant's father was not in the picture and when her grandfather came to visit, the nurse told him that she would like for him to assume the role of the father. She asked him to visit the baby every day, to talk to her and tell her that he loved her. As instructed, he talked to her and told her that he loved her every day. He also touched her with his fingertips and massaged her little hands and feet. Seeing this, the nurse said, "This baby will connect your voice with your touch, and what you are doing is going to mean as much to her survival as anything we can do here." The nurse was right; that lucky little granddaughter pulled right on through.

During World War II many children had to be cared for in orphanages. Some of them were held and touched, others, due to overcrowding and chaos, were given care without the availability of touch. The children did not get touched failed to thrive, while the others did well.

We all need to feel the power of human touch and practicing our technique is healthy. Hugs get better the more you give them, partly because every time you give you get one in return.

In conventional medicine, many physicians would never touch patients if they did not have a stethoscope. In my experience, people are hungering for a friendly touch.

Many people who would love to have a hug are afraid to initiate the process partly because they are afraid of being rejected, and partly because they have never initiated personal contact. For them it is difficult to get past their self-imposed restrictions and shyness. To be lovable one must be love-able. In order to be touchable, one must be able to touch.

Dr. Gladys explains the importance of massage from a medical and biological standpoint:

Massage is important for lymphatic drainage. It stimulates the nerves, helps coordinate the cerebrospinal and sympathetic nervous systems, and it alleviates muscle spasms. Beyond all this, human beings benefit from massages because we have a need to be touched by loving, caring hands. Babies benefit from loving and caring touch and as we age it continues to be important to give and receive love and caring in the form of touch.

Sadly, many of us are so unaccustomed to touch that we have become afraid of our own bodies. Furthermore I think, in our focus on disease, we may have done real damage to many women by telling them to regularly check their breasts FOR LUMPS. I have patients who are so afraid of finding lumps that they never touch their own breasts if they can help it. Others seem to check for lumps over and over, until I think the breast says, "Oh, she wants lumps, perhaps we should produce some." I am not saying that we should not check our breasts, only that they are not our enemies. Could we not love them and gently feel them, while asking, "Hello, Girls, do you have a message for me?" I know my breasts will let me know if I need to know anything about them.

We learn more from our bodies if we love, honor and treat them with respect.

Chapter 21
Consequences

It may not ever look like we do, but Old Ladies pause. Since I have learned how to pause, I have discovered many benefits. Pause, listen; your heart will show you the way to accept the things you cannot change.

Dr. Gladys had one of her grandsons on her lap; it was her 70th birthday and they were in her favorite rocking chair. Daniel had heard about grandmothers in the many stories his mother had read to him. He was making a connection, beginning to appreciate the value of having his grandmother nearby and available. As he pondered the mystery of her, questions began to arise.

"Nanni, why is your skin like that?"

"I am seventy, Daniel."

"Is that old?"

"I don't know, Daniel. Some people think it is old."

"Well, I am four, and when you get really, really old and you get to be really, really sick, I am going to go up to your room and I am going to pick you up in my arms and I am going to rock you, and rock you, and rock you."

Stories like these, arising from close associations with our elders, are instruction in the things children need for mental, emotional and spiritual development. A child who sees loved ones getting older from day to day develops a priceless natural acceptance of the life process. Such children grow up knowing that wrinkles bring to the surface what years have brought to the heart and soul. They know wrinkles are hard earned marks of the wisdom acquired by accumulated experiences. They know we have the right to trust and honor our truth. It is disheartening when women are hesitant to embrace their wisdom and its emblems.

When Daniel was young, he and his brother would look at my face and rub it, trying to get rid of the "wrunkles", as they called them. I told them to leave them alone. I deserve every wrunkle that I have; I have worked hard for them.

Even though we may not be able to do what we chose to do when we were younger, the work an Old Lady chooses to do in old age deserves to be valued for the support it offers humanity. Regardless of her origins and her chosen life work, each of our world's Old Ladies are the roots and the life force that began at her birth, and every one of the seasons of her life has rich gifts to offer. The advantages of traveling the course of life into old age is that it comes with opportunities to share life's wisdom with others.

In the Native American culture, elders speak of Mother Earth and the necessity of respecting and honoring the ground we walk on. They call fossil fuel extracted from the deep, the blood of Mother and they fear the effect of Man's greed on life and land.

Unfortunately, we often dismiss such stories and beliefs, unable to reconcile them with our dedication to the scientific approach which has shaped modern life. Although science does not seem to back them up yet, there are numerous instances where the passage of time has enabled science to pick up where the story ended, where the old stories have merged with new science. In that light, some of those tales are akin to prophecies.

Suni, is a long time friend, dear to Dr. Gladys. Introducing her nephew from Germany to the exclusively American experience of Hopi and Navajo culture, she took him to northern Arizona. The smog over Phoenix was impossible to ignore and his notice of it led to a story about Bitter Waters and how they came to be.

The old women of the two tribes told him about a large mining company, so agressive in its efforts to strip and mine for coal and uranium that the liver of Mother Earth became damaged. Taking long breaths between sentences and stories, these old ladies of the Hopi and Navajo lands explained the relation between Mother Earth and themselves.

As greedy companies and their employees dug up the land, they promised better lives to the people, but they were obviously damaging Mother Earth's lungs. Tribal people themselves began having troubles with their own breathing after returning from work in the mines, experiencing problems with their lungs. The people became sick and the drinking water became bitter as the mine recklessly damaged the vital organs of Mother Earth. Pointing to the haze on the horizon the old women blamed the miners' greed. Although science uses different terminology, it is now validating the damage to the earth caused by the reckless and discompassionate greed of humans.

I was hosting some people from a remote area of New Zealand as they were visiting Sedona, Arizona. I walked with an Old Lady, enjoying a day of nature in an environment quite different from that of her native land. She was bent with age and, wanting to explore where others more nimble had walked, had purchased a long stick made of the rib of a cactus plant. After the first step with her stick, she said it helped her with balance and she felt more flexible.

She may have had trouble with balance, but this old lady was an expression of gratitude for life itself. We walked toward a tattered sign and through an orchard. She touched the trunk of an apple tree and caressed the fruits. At rhythmical intervals, she took long breaths as if to take in what these trees had to offer and at times she stopped to examine some of the exposed roots.

A short while later she turned to me and said, "Did you know that plants, particularly trees, are the lungs of the earth? You see, the rocks, the earth itself and the water on the ground and under our feet allow the trees to inhale a special, necessary kind of spirit of life, and then, through transpiration, they release something beneficial to our lives. The leaves of every tree tell a story; you should try breathing sometime."

We continued our walk, picked some apples and did not speak of the inspiration or exhalation of trees or people, but the seed of the idea that she planted was growing and I was becoming conscious every breath I took.

In 2012, scientists in Australia, from Queensland University of Technology, seem to have come to a similar conclusion. In their laboratories they found that wooded areas have twice the concentration of positive and negative ions in their air than areas with little vegetation. I read further that radon, a water soluble by-product of the radioactive decay of radium in the earth, occurs in small quantities, in rocks which, in turn continually exude radon. Trees are incredibly effective pumps and filters, absorbing water, nutrients, and toxins like radon, utilizing, and detoxifying them efficiently as they are transported to the rest of the organism. Through the transpiration occurring in the leaves trees are able to release into the atmosphere that which does not serve them. Things that do not serve them include neutralized radon as well as oxygen.

This Old Lady's idea was affirmed by scientific research. Hopefully there will come a time when people and large companies will hold hands in harmonious cooperation for optimal consequences.

The World Needs Old Ladies

Chapter 22
Food for Thought

Food preferences are closely connected to our cultural and family heritage. Much of our personality, our beliefs, our likes and our dislikes are expressed in or reinforced by the food we eat. We associate the foods we love with our memories of good times. The foods we know are the ones we like and it is easy to spoil our taste buds by limiting their experiences to familiar or addictive foods. Although it is as much of a challenge to change dietary habits as it is to adapt to another culture or to learn a new language, refusal to address unhealthy food choices is a serious threat to our well-being.

Our food is the fuel our body needs for proper function. Every cell in our body depends on receiving nutrients from the food choices that we make.

The minute we put food into our mouths, saliva mixes with it and starts the digestive processes. When we eat hurriedly and do not take time to chew, or when we drink water to wash our food down, the saliva does not have a chance to start this process properly. It is not fair to ask the stomach to do a job for which it is not prepared and not equipped.

The digestive juices in the stomach are there for the next stage of digestion and when the food enters the small intestine, it is further mixed with the digestive juices of the pancreas and the liver. If the food receiving this treatment is not properly prepared for this process, fermentation and gas is the frequent result.

Although diet is a very personal thing and what one person likes another dislikes, our body has certain dietary needs that we will meet if we are wise. It is important that we eat as many fresh fruits and vegetables as our body can handle, that our breads are primarily made of whole grain and that we have proteins for building our muscles and bones. This does not necessarily have to be animal protein, and people who choose to be vegetarian can have very good protein intakes from legumes, tofu, nuts, sunflower seeds and a variety of other substances. Milk and milk products are not always the best source of protein because frequently, as we get older we have trouble digesting them. Yogurt and buttermilk are better choices.

Not only do each of us have our own likes and dislikes when it comes to foods, we also have our own tolerances and intolerances, sensitivities and allergies. Some folks need more salt, some need no salt, some need spices to stimulate their gastric juices, while others cannot tolerate spices.

The more we are able to take pleasure and delight in the food we eat, the more acceptable it is to the body and the more easily it is digested. It is important, therefore, that we make our mealtime a time with as much happiness as we can create. The act of blessing our food enhances the food itself and allows us to take in what is blessed; it benefits us on many levels to bless the foods that we eat and to be grateful for every morsel we digest. An attractive presentation also makes food more acceptable to us, and therefore more readily digested. Even the attitude we have while we are eating affects the way our food is digested and utilized. People who are grateful for what they have and who take in their food with joy and happiness can thrive on very poor diets. The diet of the coolies who carried me up the Himalyan mountains was not a balanced diet, but their bodies received it and used it well, having adapted to and being grateful for it. Other more affluent people may be unable to utilize excellent diets because anxiety has interfered with the flow of their digestive juices, preventing even the best of food from being digested well.

The attitude of the person preparing the meal also has an effect on the food. Whether we are cooking for ourselves or for others, it is good to maintain a positive and creative attitude so that the food best satisfies us, physically and emotionally.

How much time do you take to eat a meal? Do you take the time to chew each mouthful? How important is it to you to have a pleasant atmosphere at mealtime? How often do you get into an argument around the dinner table?

After reading the questions above I was brought back to the ancestral homes of my family. For the people of France, for those from the Mediterranean areas and for many other wise and fortunate people, eating is a leisurely and sensory experience. The abundance of food is not what brings this pleasure it is our attitude toward the moments we have to experience nourishment that can change the mundane act of shoving food down our throats to the pleasure-filled experience of dining with good company.

Many of us too often consume our foods while we are rushed. We eat a bag of french fries, smiling while we drive away to a meeting. We accept heartburn, diarrhea and indigestion as normal parts of life. We suffer from Irritable Bowel Syndrome, colon and rectal problems, clogged arterial systems, and toxic livers and kidneys without ever we stopping long enough to ask why.

There is a very long list of concerns that affect digestion. The process begins when we start thinking about the food we will eat, not in the intestinal track. Taking a moment to bless and be grateful for the daily bread is not an empty ritual; focus and gratitude have real health value no matter how they are manifested.

On the study group nights that I am with Dr. Gladys, she often talks about being alert, present and conscious. As her friend's body knew what to do to repair broken bones, or my ruptured esophagus knew what was needed to repair itself, so our digestive system knows what it needs in order to do what it was designed to do.

Chapter 23
Communication

I was drawing and listening to an old woman talk to her grandchildren at a park where people enjoyed a beautiful day. The Old Lady noticed a man with a horse, available for a ride. She paid the attendant so her grandchildren could ride the horse, but her grandson, afraid of the palomino, cried. The gentle grandmother took him by the hand, approached the horse and lovingly caressed the horse's flank, never letting go of the boy's hand. She repeated her movements, talking softly, and telling the little boy, "When you give love as I am doing right now, the horse receives love and he feels very good; I do too. Try it. Touch him and see how it feels to you."

His crying had stopped and he cautiously touched the horse. Then he touched him again. Soon these touches became caresses similar to those of his grandmother. They both continued to caress the horse together.

This Old Lady was one of the patient people Dr. Gladys talks about. Her ideal led her to an idea, and she found the way to get her grandson on that horse. Before my drawing was done, I saw the boy riding the horse; he looked proud of himself. I approached her and asked how she had accomplished such a complete reversal in the boy's perception. "With patience, dear, you can do almost anything."

Not long ago there was a lot of concern over a flu epidemic. On a Sunday morning I went into a church where the practice of "Sharing the Peace" was a weekly tradition during which members of the congregation turned to each other and shook hands or gave each other a hug. On this particular Sunday morning I was surprised to see that many of the people were either just nodding to each other or were wearing gloves to shake hands. The reason few of them were honestly embracing and making contact with other people, of course, was that they were afraid to catch the flu. I was struck by the irony of the situation. The church, which is a sanctuary for love and healing, had become a place where people were afraid of each other, afraid of the very people with whom they shared a loving, caring and spiritual communion. While the communication of love and caring were expressed in sermons and rituals, this behavior, sadly, expressed only fear.

When my oldest son was a two-year-old toddler running around playing in and out of the dirt, a physician friend of mine had a son of the same age. She kept her son in little white gloves and would not let him play in the dirt. She constantly watched over him so he didn't hurt himself or didn't get into anything that was dirty. Her little fellow was sick most of the time. My son, on the other hand, with his scrapes and bruises, was healthy. The difference was that bacteria did not scare me; they were not my enemy or the enemy of my son.

In the Smithsonian Magazine of July and August, 2010,

there is a remarkable article entitled "Listen to Bacteria" about a microbiologist named Bonnie Bassler. For the past sixteen years Bonnie Bassler has been at the forefront of the fast growing field of "quorum sensing" which is the study of how microbes communicate with each other. To use today's language, Bassler is comparing the way in which news hounds now utilize communication devices glued to their Cell phones and Internet chat lines to bacterial communication. Bacterial communication is a complex chemical language in which molecules are able to alert one another through chemical signaling. Tiny bacterial cells can band together and perform the work of giants. Bassler has discovered that there are two distinct styles of communication in the world of bacteria. One is species specific, understandable only by bacteria of the same kind. The other uses a sort of multilingual dialogue. We are used to thinking of bacteria communicating with their own kind, but she has opened up the possibility that inter-species communication is a part of the quorum-sensing story.

As a multilingual individual I see the normalcy of such discovery. I speak one tongue with my own people, and use other languages or codes to speak with others. Since I am a juxtaposition of millions of cells, why would they not operate as I do? I am part of them, like a leaf on the tree.

Bacterial species are able to communicate effectively with each other, and this discovery changes scientific perception. Instead of language as we know it, bacteria signal molecules and are able to measure the number of the molecules within a population. This phenomenon enables a single cell to sense the number of bacteria by means of the accumulation of its signaling molecules. Bacteria understand cell density. Many different bacteria live together using various classes of signaling molecules. They cannot talk to all other bacteria any more than I can speak all the languages of the various people in my immediate environment but quorum sensing enables bacteria to co-ordinate their behavior.

Bacteria need to respond quickly in order to survive. They must adapt both to nutrients, and to the presence of toxic and dangerous compounds. Quorum sensing studies have been able to shed new light on the use of antibiotics, and understanding nature has become very practical in this recent work.

The antibiotics we have been using for many years are geared toward killing bacteria. Since all living substances have the innate programming of survival, bacteria have become more resistant to the antibiotics that are being used to kill them. New antibiotics are constantly being developed to kill the bacteria that have outsmarted the antibiotics and become resistant to them, but the cycle keeps repeating.

Dr. Bassler has found that by changing the focus from killing bacteria to interfering with their ability to communicate with each other, the growth of the bacteria can be controlled; therefore, the growth of disease can also be controlled, even eliminated.

This incredibly important research shows that as long as a group of bacteria are communicating with their own species, not calling in help from other bacterial species, they are contained within the body they have a symbiotic relationship with. If something happens, if there is a trigger and signals are sent out to other groups of bacteria, there can be a response to the calls; the bacteria become virulent, and disease manifests. It seems that in order for the disease to become a reality, bacteria need the help of other species. If they have no way of communicating with others, the numbers do not accumulate and the disease does not develop.

The implications of this research constitute a quantum leap in our understanding of bacterial behavior. Isn't it wonderful that it all comes down to communication!

The Gospel of John starts with, "In the beginning was the word and the word was with God, and the word became flesh and dwelt among us." In other words, "the word" or communication is the essence of life itself. Communication goes on at the most basic level of life, which is vibration. All living things communicate in some way with other living things and communication is necessary for life to continue.

Within our bodies, we have adult stem cells that are constantly regenerating tissues and replacing cells that have become damaged or have died. These adult stem cells are not the embryonic cells that have caused so much concern and controversy. Embryonic cells are not usable; they can create tumors and they are extremely difficult to culture out. Adult stem cells, on the other hand, are constantly circulating within our body, always in the process of reconstructing tissue.

There is work now being done that allows for the collection of adult stem cells from a person's body. In a biopsy, stem cells can be removed, cultured out into undifferentiated stem cells and reintroduced into a person's body when there has been tissue damage such as that which occurs in heart attacks. These stem cells then somehow communicate with the differentiated cells surrounding them, able to thereby transform themselves into re-differentiated cells, say of the heart, regenerating it.

"First there was the word, and the word became flesh." This Bible quotation seems to be, in fact, the communicative method by which transformation takes place in adult stem cells. Our cells, sick or otherwise are as talkative as mockingbirds. They have the power of imitation; place them in the right environment and they sing vigorously. We are working with this knowledge to the benefit of our health. Now we are finding that even microbes have consciousness and are capable of communication; we are just beginning to see how this can also be used to our benefit.

As individuals, when we communicate love and healing to our body, we strengthen the stem cells born to keep our immune system active and functional; as scientists we can put the stem cells to work for us even more, and we have hope of disrupting the adaptive microbial communication that facilitates their ability to defeat our present defenses. If, on the other hand, we live in fear, turning at first threat to antibiotics, I believe we give pathological bacteria a direct line to other bacteria which can enhance their activity, so that pathologies evolve.

The fear of those people in church led them to similarly ineffective means of protection. Life is complicated, we might as well live it; there don't seem to be any provable benefits to avoiding it.

If the concept of living medicine is that life itself is the great healer, and if life is the great communicator, then communication must also be a great healer. Since healing and hurting both take about the same amount of energy, perhaps the choices we make, the thoughts we harbor, the communications we send and receive deserve our most careful consideration.

The World Needs Old Ladies

Chapter 24
My Healing

Many years ago, I was in a hospital ready to take my last breath. Doctors worked with the best tools available to them in their search for a diagnosis without which they would be unable to give me the support I needed. I personally didn't care about a diagnosis; I just wanted to help my body take care of the problem. We were not on the same page.

There is often confusion in the interactions between doctors and patients. Their perspectives are different; their educations are different, their language is different; and their goals are different. One does not easily understand the world of the other. I had been close enough to Dr. Gladys to know that deep inside me there was a physician I could call on. She had explained where some of her approaches came from. I began to educate myself in them and I found answers that were right for me. Dr. Gladys had experienced a shift in her medical approaches when she realized that there was much in the field of medicine which had not been taught in medical school.

It was very difficult to understand how I could change my approach to diseases. From my training in medicine, I knew to look for a diagnosis of the specific disease and for a therapy that would help to treat that disease.

This new approach to healing did not fit the model. Its focus was not on the disease, but on the person, and on physiological principles that were inherent in maintaining health. I had to start thinking about balance, about balance within the body, between the kidney and the liver, the heart and the lungs. I had to consder the collaboration between the sympathetic and the parasympathetic nervous systems. The approach made sense. I understood the importance of the lymphatic system. The more familiar I became with this work, the more I liked what I learned; I began to look at my patients as whole people, not as disease-ridden bodies.

When I finally was able to comprehend that the use of the castor oil pack for problems as divergent as epilepsy or a sprained ankle had to do with the way the lymph traveled through the body, I found that it was also related to vibration and energy. I continued to identify diseases, but I began to treat individual people, and I found there was a great deal more to it than recognizing disease.

I learned that forgiveness breaks the bonds that hold us to blocked energy that causes illness. The Chinese say that pain comes from the chi energy being blocked and that acupuncture allows it to flow again,thus relieving the pain. I learned that castor oil packs clear the lymphatic system so that the lymph can flow without obstruction.

I began to wonder why in the Bible, as far as I know, the only diseases mentioned are leprosy and epilepsy. Jesus didn't seem to treat diseases. I came to believe that one of the reasons many ancient therapies are so complicated is because working with them requires so much patience, persistence and consistency. One has to look way beyond the "fix-it" consciousness.

I also needed to learn what it means to make a mistake. Most of us spend enormous amounts of time and energy worrying about our perceived mistakes. That energy is wasted unless you realize what amazing instructors mistakes are. Now I know that when you make a mistake, you have met a teacher. Some of the lessons are hard and sometimes there are casualties left behind. When you know that you have given it your best, even though you perceive that you made a mistake, maybe the lesson was for those around you. Yours was a matter of learning to accept. Trust that you have learned something.

I had to digest this. The idea that all my mistakes were my teachers gave me great pause. We process life through some natural miracle, and we can only do the best that we can with the tools we have at hand..

Wisdom is like a pearl. An oyster is not born with a pearl inside. A pearl takes a grain of sand, an irritation, a secretion and time; only then can an oyster's shell open up and offer a pearl. Listening, processing, learning from mistakes, I now know there are no ticking internal clocks waiting to strike the hour of wisdom. We all must feel the irritations of life to produce a pearl.

A few years ago, I woke up to a brilliant day, and all that was right in my life. A few hours later I got thirsty for something warm so I warmed up a cup of broth I had made. My cup of broth promised to be nourishing and easy to prepare while my husband was out. I rarely use a microwave so I carefully tested the broth to be sure it was safe temperature before I drank it. I took a sip.

Every step we take requires us to choose how we will proceed. This foot instead of that foot, forward or backward, and so life goes. Most of the time we are not conscious of the choices we make, nor why.

I took a sip of the broth and I felt an eruption somewhere in the middle of my throat. I coughed and blood, my blood, came gushing out of my mouth, and it came with extreme pain! Well trained, by media, I dialed 911. An operator answered immediately; she sounded balanced; her voice did not sound young.

Sick gurgling sounds came out of me, but no words. Blood and more blood, my blood! The old operator, well trained I must say, devised a method to communicate. She needed to know if I had been shot. I wasn't shot and I hadn't attempted suicide, but I couldn't tell her that. We communicated by me tapping on the phone, one tap for yes, and two for no, and she instructed me to open my front door if I could.

I could do that and I did, all the while coughing and leaving a trail of blood behind me. That day I understood the word panic, yet I was able to follow instructions. Panic or not, the instinct to live is a strong one.

When the army of paramedics arrived, they were men and women who seemed each to be at least seven feet tall. They immediately called my husband and transported me to the hospital. After what seemed an eternity of extreme pain I was diagnosied with a ruptured esophagus. My husband and I were told that this condition was not conducive to life.

Although I was sedated, I did not fail to understood the fragility of life, especially since it was mine. A surgeon came to explain the nature of the surgery and recovery to us. She just seemed to love saying, "Fifty-fifty." I was sufficiently aware of the severity of what had happened to me to decide what my choices were.

I decided to allow my body to heal. I had been a patient of Dr. Gladys, I had read her book, *The Physician Within You,* and I was determined to put the theory to a test.

Upset with the decision I wrote on the pad I used for communication, the surgeon left my room, mumbling something I could not understand. My husband accepted my decision with tenderness and understanding. We held hands and as the doses of morphine took effect, the pain seemed to lessen. I was unable to talk. Aside from the extreme pain that accompanied effort, a strange sound, as if from the bottom of the sea, was all that came out of my throat.

I recognized that day, that my life was not necessarily under my control, but I could not convince myself that the surgeon had much more control than I did. Healing requires a certain state of mind. I could reflect and I could affirm, "Not my will but Thy will be done," but I was not comfortable with the surgeon's approach.

It was imperative for me to change the feeling I had for this doctor and I was able to make peace when I understood and accepted that she was only acting the way she was trained. Since I could not change that, I was left only the option to change my perspective. I had to understand my own state of fear and my own wish to live.

Next, I had to have a talk with my body. Though I did not really understand about a ruptured esophagus, I knew what this organ was and what the function of this part of my body was. I became very serene, very accepting, "at peace" one might say, and I suggested to my body that I would prefer it to heal. At the same time, I was also able to make peace with the idea that my life was a temporary contract I had made with my maker.

This healing took a little more than three weeks in a hospital. I received intravenous blood and fluids with a cocktail of vitamins; paper and pencil was my mode of communication. After the third week, another battery of testing revealed that no air was escaping from my esophagus: it had healed!

Trauma has a way of presenting various sides of life. Once it was determined that the break in the esophagus had healed, I was to test it with a sip of water. The water went down uneventfully and the doctors soon suggested clear broth. Within an hour it was lunch time and a tray appeared. Surprisingly, the attendant had brought me a sandwich. With my handy pad and pencil, I reminded him that I was on a clear liquid diet. The poor man was visibly embarrassed, and told me he would return with my lunch.

After about three tries to get it right, the hospital nutritionist marched into my room to find out why I was being so difficult, why I did not want a sandwich or some mashed potatoes and chicken. My paper was still available and I simply showed it to her. "Clear Liquids Only – Vegetarian " was also written on the board that bore my name. I found out that day how imperative it is that we treat life with some humor.

A few years later, when it was time for my check up with the gastroenterologist, he told me it was impossible to have survived such an injury without surgery. The documentation from the hospital was in his hand, but he refused to believe it. I had to submit to a camera down my throat. When it was all said and done, still puzzled, he said,

"I don't understand, how did you do it?" "I talked to my body and after that, I practiced acceptance." This doctor reminded me that he was a scientist, and that science did not approve of such methods. As our conversation ended, he was smiling with a puzzled look.

Dr. Gladys offers her patients great sets of tools. Today, I believe healing can happen under the most unusual circumstances. I also know I had to rethink and relearn the meaning of the word. It is not the absence of disease that makes the difference in a life; it is working with the disease. Accepting what is known about a particular disease or condition, and going beyond that to access my physician within is what worked for me.

A dear old friend reminded me to do the work and to stay out of the result department. It was only after a ruptured esophagus that I fully understood this simple principle, often nearly impossible to achieve. The awareness that forces change is not always understood or seen. Yet, no matter what it is called, it is always there within us, ready to bring about the best outcome.

Dr. Gladys continues to remind us that being alive is a privilege granted by God. She knows what she is talking about, but for certain, I now know!

The World Needs Old Ladies

Chapter 25
The Aging Brain

My mother had the measles when she was a young girl. It was a severe case that left her deaf in one ear. If that was not enough, she was left with very poor eyesight. Beth also acquired malaria, smallpox, gallbladder problems, dysentery and finally, as she got older, severe osteoporosis and polycythemia vera. She had more than her share of conditions and ailments, yet throughout the years she never saw herself as a victim. She was grateful for every day of her life, and was one of the happiest people I have ever known.

There is an attitude of heart and soul in some people that shows they are not the problems they have. They are not stopped from doing what they feel needs to be done. Her daughter is like that too. Mothers have a way of teaching their children what they live.

Dr. Gladys knows there are things that must be done, such as allowing another to write words she has spoken because she is busy with other things. She knows about priorities and has learned to prioritize.

In the final years of my mother's life, her heart was so severely damaged that when I listened to it with my stethoscope, it was difficult to pick up a pattern. I observed that her love and compassion were so great that her physical heart had to keep going in order for her to manifest the love and compassion that were part of her spiritual heart.

Her life was never easy. She almost died when I was born, going into labor at theTaj Mahal in Agra, India. Of her five children, three were born under the Indian sky. During the winter we lived in tents in the Jungle. Primitive accommodations were the conditions she found in which she could do her life's work. The love of her God, her love of her family and of the human race, no matter who they were, gave root to her own tree of life. Humor and compassion were its fruits.

Dr. Gladys was given the article parphrased below by her daughter-in-law, Dr. Barbara McGarey. It was a research study being done at John Hopkins Hospital, based on the aging brain.

When the elderly begin to experience memory loss, they often assume that they are developing Alzheimer's disease, but research does not support that conclusion. As young people, we focus our attention on details like remembering the names, numbers, and the numerous details of our daily life. Our brain remembers that which is important in our life at the time and the aging brain has different priorities, no longer needing to retain information that is available from outside sources. With age we realize that our experiences, the lessons we've learned, the perils we've survived have changed our circumstances, enriched our perspective and re-ordered our priorities. As our years accumulate, it is natural for wise acceptance to replace the storage of details that no longer serve us. There is comfort in adjusting to the differences that occur in our lives as we age.

Unfortunately in most western cultures, the commercialization of anti-aging remedies has robbed the older generations of the gifts they have to offer. Men want to keep the status, virility, fortunes and reputation of their youth. Women want to keep their appeal, their beauty, and their growing children.

I know a ninety-four year old woman who exemplifies the damage this can cause. She lives alone but two, well-intentioned, compassionate women care for her. Her main focus, her complaint and her biggest desire is to find a facial cream that will take away her wrinkles. No one else cares about her wrinkles, but she is so fixed on the need to look young that she can talk of nothing else. In her fixation she has isolated herself from friends and family and opportunity to live fully and, as a result, she is very unhappy.

In many other cultures it is taken for granted that changes that occur with aging are natural, necessary, respectable and desirable. Buddhism maintains that change is inevitable and that suffering is the result of the attempt to avoid change through attachment to the way things are. Letting go of temporary things sounds simple, but it isn't. When a culture promotes non-attachment, it promotes enjoyment of the moment in which we find ourselves, rather than grieving over the moment we have just lost. It opens the door to contentment and contentment is a channel through which blessings flow. Cooperation into operation is found in all of nature. When I see a rose in bloom, I know the time to enjoy her scent and her beauty is right now.

In contrast to the ninety-four year old described above,

Dr. Gladys's mother was content, able to open the door to the moment in which she was living. She was that rose that allows scent, beauty and blessings to flow through her to others.

Chapter 26
The Healing Power of Dreams

For many of us, dreaming is something that happens when we are wide-awake when we are wishing for something. We daydream about a new yellow Cadillac in the driveway, or we daydream of a lake full of fish. Such wide awake dreams, day dreams, are simple fantasies concocted by conscious desires. The dreams we have when our conscious mind is out of the way are much different.

These other dreams are the ones able to offer us guidance. Albert Einstein said, "The intuitive mind is a sacred gift. The rational mind is a faithful servant. Society honors the servant and has forgotten the gift." Intuitive dreams tell us what to look for in our lives. Dreams are amazing "incubators" that help us solve problems and shed light on our untapped potential, and we all can learn from them. Dr. Gladys acts upon this concept every time a dream comes to her. She pays attention, analyzes and recognizes what is coming from the unconscious to the conscious.

A person's way of dreaming is as individual as are fingerprints, and the information we get through dreams can be used to predict illness, and to help heal the body. They often sound the first warning about pending illness or injury, and as you work with your dreams you will discover your own personal images for illness and recovery.

One woman dreamed of a fierce, roaring lion in a back bedroom of her home. When the roaring became too loud, she opened the door and threw a big piece of cheddar cheese to the lion. When I asked her how she interpreted the dream, she said she thought there was a potentially dangerous illness, possibly hypoglycemia, which could be controlled by eating more protein.

We need not be afraid of dreams. They come from many different levels of our subconscious, yet they seem to tailor their content to what the dreamer can handle. Once we learn to pay attention to and correctly interpret our dreams, we discover a partnership and begin to trust our intuition. New things, such as blossoms on trees, a new building being constructed, new clothes being tried on, or driving a car well on a dangerous mountain road are dream images that often indicate returning health.

In dreams like these our subconscious opens doors for us; not the doors of the yellow Cadillac, but the doors of our potential. Having heard, "there are no accidents", I have found that my dreams are no accidents either; they are voices that I need to listen to. They are tools provided for my use, but first I must learn to use the tools.

Recalling your dreams is not difficult. Basically you need only to suggest to yourself, as you drop off to sleep, that you will dream and be able to recall the dreams.

The first thing upon waking, accept and value each dream, no matter how foolish it seems. If your dream reaches consciousness at all, it very likely contains an important message.

Recording the dream and examining it for meaning is important. Upon waking up from a dream, write it down otherwise you will forget it. Start with whatever you can remember; even fragments are important. Know that dream recall will improve the more action you take. The physician within seems to say, "Oh, she/he is really listening. I guess it's okay to keep sending messages." Doesn't a good listener encourage all of us to speak up?

Interpretation is a matter of weighing the dream content with more familiar aspects of your life and thoughts, and acting on your dream information is vital. Working with dreams is much like learning to play a piano. You improve with practice; with more practice you may earn the title of "*Pianist*."

Dreams are powerful guides for helping us understand our health needs, and for discovering our true path. Work with your dreams. It opens up a whole new world, your world. It is exciting, fun and lets you know about yourself in a safe and personal way. Don't be afraid to share them with others who are interested. You don't need to be an expert; you just need to open your conscious mind to the voice of your deeper self.

As we age we *each develop our own sleep pattern which will be subject to change according to our needs. Unless there is some real pathology we do not need to medicate ourselves into sleep.*

I have found that there are times when I need actual sleep and there are times when what I need is down time rather than more sleep. I love going to bed whether I get a full night's sleep or not. Down time is good too. Wakeful parts of the night can be very special times; the rest of the world is sleeping, all is quiet, and I have only myself to communicate with. My moments of down time are precious moments. Sometimes I have lots on my mind; sometimes I solve problems, sometimes I'm inspired; sometimes I'm just awake. Now I have a choice to make.

This is really good prayer time for me and I treasure it. Why spend the time recalling painful memories or worrying about the fact that I'm not sleeping, when can I spend it in prayer, recall hymns I remember, or relive wonderful memories?

Unless there is some real pathology we do not need to medicate ourselves into sleep. I resent being told that my age requires a given number of hours of a certain kind of sleep each night, and I refuse to worry myself into prescription drugs for sleep. I work out my own sleep pattern and sleep when I feel the need.

A friend of mine is in her eighties and for the last few years has been concerned about a problem. She is a quilter and loves quilting, but found that frequently she would fall asleep while she was working. She began to question whether she should drive more than short distances and then she received her answer. While she was visiting her son in Minnesota she did not have the problem of waking up every hour. Her son is a doctor and suggested that she was suffering from sleep deprivation due to lack of REM sleep and asked her to think about what was different in her son's home and her own. She is a very thoughtful person and realized that when she slept in Minnesota the room was completely dark and here in Arizona there was a street light which shone into her bedroom. When she cane home she fixed the problem and was able to shut out the street light and sleep in the dark. She no longer falls asleep during the day and wakens only once or twice during the night. She is not afraid to drive and even her balance is better.

When we recognize that we have a health issue if we examine our life and how we are living it, we frequently can make some correction and solve the problem. Sometimes we get the answer in dreams and sometimes something is said or done which brings us the answer. Medication is the last answer not the first.

PART 6
The Blossoms

    Both scientifically and spiritually, everything in the universe serves a purpose and has a function. The function of life on this planet is to continue to survive.

    Blossoms; sexy, colorful and perfumed, are essential to reproduction. Although they predate us, as are part of the natural world we are attracted to the colors, diverse forms, and scents of blossoms. They stimulate our senses and we carry their pollen, helping them to form fruit, to seed and to reproduce.

Chapter 27
Flowers of Health

That which has served us for a long time is not necessarily needed forever. The reality is that life takes only what it needs from the past to engage the present and to allow the new to emerge. This is a principle that we find in all aspects of life, much like Old Ladies who take from the past, are engaged in the present, and help us emerge as better human beings.

I packed my things into a suitcase that had served me well for at least ten years. It had traveled in and out of many different countries and was ready for the trip to Washington D.C., or so I thought. Like many things we have come to take for granted, I had no plans to change my suitcase. It, however, did have other plans; it needed some change.

When I arrived in Pittsburgh, which was my first stop, I found that the zipper on my suitcase had pulled apart. I was amazed that I had not lost anything, but I did need to replace my suitcase with one more able to accommodate my coming decades of travel. I thought this was an interesting metaphor for the healthcare proposals that I was carrying to the nation's capitol in that the material I was taking back to Washington was in an overloaded suitcase similar to overload of our healthcare system. Changing needs require new delivery systems. Our country is in need of change, of a completely new way of looking at our healthcare delivery, just as I needed a change of suitcases to carry my ideas to its capitol.

As holistic caregivers, we are working toward empowering the individual, helping each person seeking heathcare to work with and understand the physician within. We support the responsibility for our own healthcare with the understanding that we are the ones who can, with the cooperation of our healthcare providers, bring about the healing within our bodies.

Urgent measures are needed to curb health costs without costing our nation's health. The creation of Centers for Community Advancement could provide health education forums for individuals, families and groups to promote wellness with the understanding that health encompasses all of life. Improvement of our individual states of health will surely reduce the costs of healthcare. Focus on personal behaviors and solutions that positively impact nutrition, obesity, hypertension, heart disease and chronic pain needs to be addressed as do daily necessities of earning a living and subsisting in the real world. By providing communities with reasonably priced educational programs that sustain the maintenance of one's health through family strength and aging into health, the country can expect to see greater productivity, a healthier population, and a significant decrease in healthcare costs.

The Center would include a Conscious Birthing Center to provide prenatal and empowering birthing services. Our present healthcare system is broken by its regard for the natural *progress of pregnancy as a disease, necessitating its treatment as a disease. This escalates the cost of childbirth and does not improve the outcome. The manner in which a child comes into the world matters, and our current birthing norm is violent enough to generate further violence in the lives of those who are subjected to it. Womb health equals world health. This center for life's initial experience can set the tone for a healthy community as it improves the efficacy and economic benefit of providing maternity services through the birthing center model.*

Staffed by carefully selected physicians, nurse practitioners, and midwives, to provide quality care to local populations. All laboring women who present at the Birthing Center would be provided care. It will be culturally sensitive, respecting each woman's cultural and religious beliefs. In the event of complications, it would be equipped and prepared to offer emergency care to the mother and baby until it is safe to transport them to the appropriate hospital.

For some unknown reason, when I was a girl in Europe and the United States a pregnant woman hid her pregnancy. It was not proper for the world to know that a woman was pregnant and she did not appear in public once the pregnancy became apparent. In India loose clothing hid the pregnancy for many months.

Things have changed. We now have clothing that shows the pregnancy, and women are happy and proud to have the pregnancy photographed. This is as it should be, pregnancy is a beautiful time of life, promising new life both for the baby born and the woman who becomes its mother.

There is great beauty in every phase of this aging process. Life and its experiences show on our bodies and faces. Rather than being ashamed of these changes, we are entitled to age beautifully into a stronger health by using our deeper roots.

In the caves of our grandmother's heart, there is hidden wisdom to guide our journey to the other side of technology. In a world that depends on devices where multitasking is a code of honor, we must reclaim the essence of what it is to be a beautiful woman.

We must relearn appreciation of our gifts. We must be able to see ourselves as we really are; our lives are rich with laughter and tears, with our devotion to our children, whether we have born them or they have other mothers. We are the sanctuary and the solace for both our children and our mates. We can be physically fragile, yet have the strength of bulls.

Women do not need statistics to know the wisdom of their grandmothers. They know their journey will take them to that wisdom, no matter what route they take. As women age and gain wisdom they deal with the bumps in the road, let go of illusions and embrace their true beauty.

Being born as a woman is a gift. We come to the world with flowers in our arms, selecting our mates and mothering the next generation. Assisted by universal laws of the ancients, we are graced with an abundance of potential and with a multitude of abilities. Inheriting this cloak of wisdom, Old Ladies of the world see the urgent need for a shift in our response to the needs of society, education and medicine.

Bringing life to the next generation is no easy task, but we come from a tree with deep roots and we grow a trunk filled with acquired knowledge that supports branches strong and long. Our leaves are countless and we have no fear of shedding a few to make room for the new ones that will follow.

The World Needs Old Ladies

Chapter 28
Welcoming Consciousness

The ripening of the best fruits and seeds for our future will require a partnership deeper than we have ever experienced. Old Ladies, fragile as they may appear, are the guardians and deliverers of the seeds of awareness, holding a consciousness that will guide our future. We are responsible, not only for ourselves, but also for the generations to follow.

A life is like a well, filled with our experiences; we should be able to quench our children's thirst, but sometimes we fall short of our goal. There was a time when smoking cigarettes was fashionable. Then we learned that our lungs were not designed to process tar and nicotine and smoking became known as a bad habit, one that kills. Habits do not change easily and we can still purchase as many packs of cigarettes as we wish. In the end, each individual makes choices and changes are slow and subtle. Any change at all takes the consciousness of the need for it. Finding the means to effect the change in ourselves is often challenging. We want our children to be consciously healthy. As we become more conscious of ourselves, of our communities, countries, our planetary environment, our children will benefit The time to regain our consciousness is now.

In 1946 my career as a family physician began. World War II was declared shortly after I started medical school and my entire time in medical school was flavored and colored by the effects of war. Perhaps the resulting sense of urgency was the reason for medicine's focus on purely the physical aspect of our nature. Matters of the mind, the spirit and the soul had no place in the physical expression of medicine.

We learned all about the mechanics and maladies of conception, pregnancy and birthing, but very little thought was given to the mother's diet, and certainly not to her mental state. There was some concern that she received enough calcium and her caloric intake was monitored, but those were the the only pregnancy concerns that were relevant.

We knew almost nothing about the mother-child connection and at that time, most women smoked to relieve their stress. No one knew that the mothers were being affected, let alone that cigarette smoking was affecting the children they were carrying within.

The concept that the mother's emotions could affect the baby was considered ridiculous. The idea that the father who had impregnated the woman was connected or important to the growing baby, was out of the question. Fathers were not allowed to be present in the birthing room at a time when his child and its mother both needed his welcoming arms.

Dr. Gladys had the wisdom to realize that fathers were an integral part of a child's birth but it took her twelve years to convince the hospital to allow fathers into the birthing room. The costs of the healthcare industry's resistance to change are evidenced by both the inaccessiblity and the impersonalization of today's medical care. It will take time and energy to clarify and effect the changes necessary but we have the wisdom and tenacity to succeed.

Even the tree must wait a while before it can bloom.

Chapter 29
The Garden

I joined an organization called Gardens for Humanity because friends brought me to a planting party. I had never heard of such things, but the idea seemed like fun. I was not dressed for planting anything because to me a planting party in a garden could have been an outdoor lunch.

There are times when we do not know what to expect, yet we do not ask those who could help; usually someone of experience; perhaps an Old Lady could assist. I went to this planting party with a pocket full of excuses and no intentions of getting my hands dirty. That was not the case for many older men and women present, and the many young girls and boys.

Doing the best I could to disappear in the background I stood on a large rock looking at the people planting while my skirt, blowing in the wind, conducted an invisible orchestra. I felt my gold sandals getting splashed with mud; the kids were having fun and certainly did not care about this statue in the way of their mud.

I was in a state of consternation, and I did not know what to do. I had not driven myself to the place. My friends were having their own fun. I was stuck!

Suddenly, I felt a pull on my clean skirt; the muddied hand of a little girl was tugging on me.

" Hi, today is my birthday. I am five-years-old. I need to go to the bathroom. Can you plant my bulb for me – over there?"

She was in a rush; placed a small play shovel in my hand and a bulb in the other. With lightning speed, she was gone. I had never seen a bulb and did not know what it would become. I knew it contained the seed of something clearly important to this little person. I gathered my skirt around me and felt my haunches about to break as I lowered myself to that place 'over there'... I began to dig a hole. I knew at least this much, as I had watched the others. My little tool was not cooperating but I kept at it. An older lady, looking at me in a sympathetic or perhaps in a pathetic way, gave me a bucket of water.

"If you saturate the area with a little water, it will get softer and you will be able to dig this hard soil." I thanked her, remembering that somewhere a long time ago I had read about the healing power of GRATITUDE.

That afternoon I gained a better understanding of gratitude. It took a while, but I created a hole for the bulb to fit in. Out of thin air came another old lady, this one handed me two old plastic bowls.

" This one has a little compost in it, and this one mulch, mix them well and the nutrients will help the Gladiola to grow." I thanked her, glancing at my newly painted fingernails. I, at least knew that the bulb had a name.

Then, I recalled that my mother had an enormous garden filled with gladiolas. I had always wondered who planted them.

Now, I had this one bulb to plant.

The little girl was nowhere to be found; I had to accomplish this small task alone. A boy about ten years old suggested, "You better dig more if you want this to work; you know, we are going to have the flowers in the spring, the vegetables too!"

He did not make any attempt to help. I noticed he had a handful of his own bulbs to plant. As instructed, I dug some more.

When this venture began, at first, I felt alone. It took a short time and I became aware that I was not alone – that the little girl, the two Old Ladies, and also the boy were all aware of me. All I had to do was to stay on task.

I might have been smiling, also remembering the meaning of "patience". I dug and with my bare hands made a mixture I knew the bulb would appreciate. The bulb slipped down and was covered up, and I stood taller! The little girl reappeared, all smiles, as I handed her tools back to her.

"Thank you very much, but Johnny told me you did not know how to plant because you put the bulb upside down. Let's fix it."

That day I learned mostly not to be afraid of things foreign to my comfort zone. I also found that answers to unspoken questions often came from the most unexpected places. A couple of Old Ladies and a couple of children had been my teachers. A bulb I could have taken the time to examine, surely would have told me where its roots were for it, too, was a teacher.

Chapter 30
Tools for Life

On my meditation garden wall I still have a "Kurpe" and a Sickle from India. Village women used them as they cultivated their small fields and gardens. I remember as a small child watching them work with the kurpe. They dug and planted their crops, just as Eveline planted a bulb, and everyone experienced something magical and transformative.

When I was that young girl I would sit hunkered down on my haunches just like them, but I could not quite get the same result. When they used their hand held sickles to harvest the crop, they were so quick and so skilled that I often wondered how they managed to avoid cutting themselves.

These tools are not pretty; they are timeworn and crude, but they hold special memories. They are not about carefree times. They are the reminders of a time when women worked in the hot sun to scrape out of the earth the food they fed to their families. The saris these women wore were often ragged, but they were always colorful. The work they did was hard, but using these tools with skill, they did what they needed to do.

When we use old tools, it does not mean we settle for less. Rather, it means that we use what we have, to the best of our abilities, so that we do not become stuck. We can still be colorful and productive while we look for better tools.

By the way, the tools I speak of here, the kurpe and the sickle, which were used in the 1920s can still be used in my little meditation garden.

Now that I am an Old Lady, I know how valuable these tools were to me as a young girl; they are still of great value to me. While caring for them, they care for my needs. They are part of my bank of helpful memories. I could have thrown the tools away; if I chose to do this, I would be left with fading memories and nothing more.

Often we throw away great opportunities because we do not want to do the work it takes to keep them working. Perhaps the grand Old Ladies of the world are available to teach us to be the best that we can be.

From such small slices of life, I realize that the energy held by things we find sacred provides us with hope and healing. This also happens when seeds are planted and nurtured. This is the stuff that nourishes souls and grows the wisdom needed for generations to come.

Something beautiful happens when we do what we need to do. Dr. Gladys' mother called it "make do."

I wonder how many opportunities we have missed because we thought we had to have better tools, not realizing that if we used what we had on hand we could do the work we needed to do until the better tools came along.

Nothing escapes this changing world. In our own ways, we all tarnish; yet when polished, we still each reflect the brilliant world around us.

During late 1940s I was a young woman, I lived in Wellsville, Ohio. A friend had a baby and I gave her a silver baby cup with the baby's name engraved on it. She appreciated the gift.

Silver and shiny! It was a year later when I saw her again and she told me that the cup had gone bad. I was mystified and asked her how? "Well, it turned black so I threw it away." She did not know that silver needed to be polished in order to keep tarnish from accumulating. When not polished, the shine vanishes. Yet it is always there, beneath the tarnish.

In 1969 a group of us flew into Jerusalem arriving just as the sun was setting. As we were getting ready to land, from the small airplane's window I could see the entire city aglow.

At the center of our view was the Dome of the Rock with its beautiful huge golden dome. It is a place sacred for Jews, Christians and Muslims I noticed a similarity to our sun in its glow. It was breathtaking. Then I saw the smaller silver dome of St. Ann's Church reminding me of the moon.

We all recognize the fact that the sun and the moon have powers central to life on earth. The sun is golden and the moon is silver. The sun emits its own light while the moon emitting no light reflects the light from the sun.

Metals, gold and silver, show the attributes of sun and moon. Gold does not tarnish; its shine remains clear and pure no matter how much it is exposed to the elements. Silver, on the other hand, reacts to exposure to the elements by creating a chemical reaction that causes it to tarnish. Silver, when polished shines and reflects light; tarnish hides its light.

Gold represents the sun while silver symbolizes the moon; two metals, both reflective of our life patterns on this earth. The sun becomes the symbol of grace and the moon becomes the symbol of karma. The sun has within it the power, the flow, and the energy that shines and brings life, love and healing into our human lives. That is grace. The light of the moon comes from the sun. It does not create its own light. That is Karma.

The life experiences that accumulate in our soul are like tarnish accumulating on silver when it is exposed to the elements. When that happens the karmic patterns frequently stop reflecting the light of the sun. As a person, our shine dulls.

As we live through lifetimes we accumulate karmic patterns, habits, and thought forms. These can become so attached to how we respond to our life experiences, that they can actually tarnish our soul in a way that keeps the light of the sun from reaching the shiny silver.

When we begin to recognize that our light is not shining, and/or that the light of God is being interfered with by our responses to our environment and by our experiences, we have choices. We can work toward cleaning up these patterns, getting rid of the old tarnish and allowing the light to shine through, or we can also choose to allow the tarnish to accumulate and keep us in darkness.

The polish used to clean off this tarnish is the fruit of the spirit. It takes time to polish a soul; it takes love, kindness for self, and for others. It requires generosity and caring. It requires innumerable deeds of kindness.

It is in the act of forgiveness and the reality of hope that our soul attributes are developed. Our soul wishes to shine. Life's experiences and the choices we make sometimes cloud and cover our very response to our life experiences.

In reality, we have many tools that work as polish to clean the tarnish off. Meditation is one, prayer is one, music, dancing, massage, paying attention to our diet; these are all acts that, when we consciously work with our body, mind and spirit, allow our souls to shine forth. Furthermore, regardless of where one looks, cause and effect convey the reality that our actions influence outcome.

The idea that karma can be defined as our memory and grace as God's memory, becomes a profound statement.

We humans remember good and bad. If karma is memory, what it seems to be saying to me, is that as long as we remember the hard times, our weaknesses, the things we have done wrong, or the way others have wronged us, we continue to feed "bad" karma. In other words, as long as we feed the memories of the hurts and pain we have sustained karma continues to stay with us and is self-perpetuating.

As we change our thoughts and memories we create within ourselves the ability to create goodness.

Karma is the application of the laws of cause and effect. The idea is that if we learn, through life, to accentuate and manifest the' fruits of the spirit. We can be kind and gentle, demonstrating and bringing peace for humankind.

To change the laws of karma into the law of grace, we must begin with self, paying attention to deep-seated patterns and habits. Then we can begin to work with our various relationships, constructing with discipline an environment within us where our patterns become less consuming and our drives become simple urges.

Forgiveness is a central part of moving from karma into grace. Forgiveness of ourselves and others. First we recognize what needs to be forgiven, this is the work of the mind, and then we have to work on moving it into the heart. Until we really feel it in our heart we still have work to do. This can take a long time, and in my life has taken a lot of prayer and help from friends, family and The Holy Spirit.

I was once given a list of good ideas to initiate the path from karma to grace.

- Choose according to your ideal.
- Act according to your ideal, in tune with the spiritual laws you know and understand.
- Be creative in the little things as well as the big things.
- Give up criticizing and condemning others and yourself.
- Be not hurt by words when somebody is harsh or critical.
- Let peace enter into your life and the life of everyone that you meet.
- Forgive yourself and others. Love your neighbor as yourself.

PART 7
The Seeds and the Fruits

I think of the seeds of life, which in my life have become the old women, for they are the carriers of life's potential and they are all around us. They are us!

We Old Ladies contain the courage to grow into what we were meant to be, with the faith to face our individual challenges. We contain memories, the seeds that will continue the process of life.

Without the seeds in place, the forest would not be. The wisdom of the old would be lost in the winds. Generations would falter.

When I think of the new seeds that have been modified to produce other than what nature meant them to be, I realize our gardens face the end of the natural process. This is the place where we must tread with care.

It is also in that place that we sometimes seem to get lost. Yet, in nature we can find the beginnings of life, the best remedies to heal heart and mind, spirit and body. In that place of many fruits are many seeds, still there to help us live.

The World Needs Old Ladies

Chapter 31
The Three Immortals

Do you remember your first "baby doll", the one that looked like and felt like a baby? Did you give her a name? Did you love her? This first doll was the preparation our mothers used to teach us to become mothers. The tree of life was filled with these dolls, like flowers of various colors.

The dolls I played with as a little girl looked and dressed like babies, and little girls. When I had daughters, they also had dolls that looked and dressed like little girls. They played little girl make-believe games with them, and with their friends.

What a wondrous way this was, a long time ago, when little girls did not need to grow up faster than nature allowed. Something happened.

In the mid 1950s there was a change. Little by little, the Barbie doll took the place of the little girl dolls. By the 1960s, every little girl felt like she needed to have a Barbie doll.

Barbie was a teenager; thus, a simple baby doll was no longer enough for little girls. There was a need to grow up faster.

Barbie came with all the equipment, clothing, and sophistication of a teenager. Little girls no longer played with their baby dolls, with little girl dresses, saddle shoes and bobby socks. Barbie had glamorous dresses, high heels, and panty hose. She soon had friends and even a boyfriend.

What have we done to our daughters? Little girls? Around thirteen or so, little girls are now women competing with their mothers for the fire in the eyes of on-lookers. What have we fueled our children with and for what purpose? Have we forgotten our responsibilities toward our children?

It seems to me that we are depriving these little girls of their natural transition and growth into puberty. Instead of little tea parties, they dress up to go to fancy balls, tennis games and sophisticated swimming parties. All of this before they are even ready to start thinking about training bras!

We know that in life, growth and development are integral processes. If we force an accelerated growth, we can miss an important phase in the process. There is then a lack of development of normal cellular synaptic changes, such that are essential for children to grow into solid responsible human beings.

When we skip a time of natural growth so that we do not know who we are, then we do not know how to age with grace. We are scared of getting old, often because we were never young. We did not find who we were.

I wonder how much damage we have already done to our young women, and why in the world we would do this any way. Why do we have beauty contests for little girls? What have we done to the self-image of a nine or ten-year-old girl, who is growing fast, is uncoordinated, her hair is not what she would like it to be? She really wants to be a little girl and be who ever

194

she is. She is trying to find out who that person is. She doesn't need to be glamorous or even pretty at that age. She needs to be loved for who she is, not what she looks like.

There is sadness in my heart when I realize this to be a story that can be encountered in any village, any town, any state and in any country. At eight or ten years, little girls want to swing a bat, not their hips.

The thoughts of a young girl are more likely that boys have cooties, than that they should like to be getting ready to go on a date with Ken. Isn't it ironic that we push the little girls to grow up too fast and then spend the remaining years of our lives trying to look younger than our age? We refuse to accept that aging is part of a natural growth, and that maturity has its own aspects of beauty.

Could it be because we, as a society, are afraid to get old, so we attempt to make ourselves and our daughters the age of the newfound Barbie? The problem with this situation is that nature does not do its work using plastic models. We ignore that our lives are temporary gifts and give our attention to staying physically young, instead of giving our consideration to growing old into grace, knowledge and wisdom.

I learned not too long ago, that there is a Chinese tradition that speaks of "The Three Immortals" and they are menstruation, childbirth and menopause. We, in our "wisdom" have taken these three stages of life, our physical and spiritual heritage, and made them into diseases which we try to get rid of. We have forced the little girls into puberty, and then we spend thirty years or more trying to get rid of the menstrual cycle so that we are not inconvenienced.

We have called menstruation "the curse", and yet we are asking little girls to face this natural process before they are ready to do so.

We have made child bearing a disease that somehow needs to be treated medically. We have taken away the natural power and beauty of childbirth.

When menopause is something we would like to avoid, we treat this natural process as a disease, often with surgical implication.

When we are in the final stages of these life cycles, and able to finally access deeper wisdom, will we try to eliminate that too?

In my lifetime I have met countless women who have gone through complete hysterectomies simply because they could not be bothered with having one more period. Life is a divine gift, requiring a natural cellular synaptic growth, from conception till death. Every stage of this process has its own beauty and rewards. Lust to dust. So when we deprive ourselves of the wonder of life, which is not always comfortable, we miss the wonderful beauty and riches of life. The blooms of the tree follow the seasons, and we women also have our seasons. We can't fool Mother Nature.

Chapter 32
Thoughts Are Things

Now that I know that each one of my cells is an organism unto its own self, and I also know it is the basic unit of my life I can better understand that I am one and I am many. Like the sky above, I am a universe with stars twirling about and suns shining within me.

Each cell has its own skin to protect it, a sort of a hydro plant, to regulate the movement of water. A cell does not want a flood and does not want a drought. If you are looking at your DNA as it travels to its nucleus, check out the organelles and other parts; they are taking care of daily operations.

None of this would work if the power plant went dormant. Cells, like a new or old car need fuel, they eat and also multiply and are very grateful when I feed them correctly.

Albert Einstein said: "We cannot solve our problems with the same thinking we used when we created them." This requires a paradigm shift.

The cells of our body know their jobs. When we living human beings set our ideals to work toward the manifestation of the fruits of the spirit, our cells know what to do.

In the 1980s, Robert Becker, M.D., wrote his groundbreaking

work in the book "The Body Electric." He spoke about the use of electrical impulse to stimulate and re-grow the limbs of frogs and even of rats. He likened the electrical impulse that he used to the electrical impulse that is created through a nerve within the human body which moves the stimulation to a cell to do what it is structured to do.

I have heard, "Thoughts are things," The evolving research, mentioned above, is giving us tools with which we can manifest this basic principle in our lives.

I think when your roots are deep in the earth, and you have lived to grow tall and have branches long enough to create harbor and shade for many, you have stories to tell .

My sister-in-law is ninety-nine years old. Her age could be challenging enough to this old lady without the addition of blindness and diabetes, and plenty of wrinkles that could easily make her bitter and angry. Yet this old lady is not defined by her conditions nor by her disabilities.

Constantly singing hymns of praise, she demonstrates that she has made the choice to be a delight to those around her. She is a wonderful companion, able to teach us that no matter what happens to us, it is the choices we make and the attitude we display that determine who we are.

At the time of this story, our family was going to a wedding in Philadelphia, in a procession of different cars carrying fourteen joyous people. I was in the lead car with my brother Gordon driving, while they were busily talking, watching the scenery, then talking some more.

Gordon noticed something and said: "Oh my, there is a

dead dog." The drive continues, a while later, Gordon says, "Look, there's another dead dog." The caravan is still going on the scenic road. The time for the wedding is approaching rather fast! Gordon drives on, "Oh my, there's another dead dog, Oh no, it's the same dead dog."

By that time everyone realizes we had been driving around in circles, we are totally and royally lost. A moment goes by to gauge the next move. The other cars filled with family members wait for the leader, probably this too shall pass, they know about these things and no one panics.

From the back seat of the lead car, a sweet angelic voice begins to sing the hymn. "The Lord knows the way in the wilderness. All we have to do is to follow". The caravan arrived at the church in time, still laughing.

Singing helps sometimes when we are lost.

As I continue to observe life I laugh, because I know this is how we old ladies deal with our fears. I also know that as one listens to those that have walked further than we have, they are able to teach us what the gift of life really is.

Another old lady lived a life of pain, joy, suffering, healing and love. Her name was Helen and she died last year at the age of 96. When she was twelve years old she had poliomyelitis which left her with a body paralyzed from the waist down. This required multiple surgeries for many years, but she lived her life proud that she was able to get around on crutches, drive a special car, marry a wonderful man, have a beautiful daughter, and run her own beauty shop. Her husband died when her daughter was in high school and she was able to support herself and her daughter *running her beauty shop. She even was able to put her daughter through college and although she was still on crutches, she did not consider herself handicapped.*

Many years later, after having to deal with broken hips, many other health problems, and financial setbacks, she moved in to her daughters' home, because she needed more care. This was when she was in her nineties.

She was a person we loved to visit because she was still so much involved with life and concerned with what she could do to help others. As her mind began to loose its connection with this realm of reality, living became very hard, but a beautiful thing happened. A great-grandson was born! This little boy from the time he was able to run around, would run into Helen's room, and with her help climb up into her bed, cuddle down under her arms and tell her his story. He talked his baby talk which we could not understand and she told him what she was seeing which we could not see. They were in a world of love, all their own. How much he will remember is not important; what is important is that in this world of trouble, pain, and suffering the two of them created a point of light which brought beauty into the lives of all of us who knew and loved them.

Old Ladies are the ones who can do this!

Chapter 33
Pregnancy - The Disease

The Old Ladies of the world seem to have a clear understanding of birth and also understand the dying process, having lived long enough to have experienced and witnessed both. They know about nature and they understand what new technologies have brought to the table.

Old Ladies look at a tree, they notice its branches spreading wide and far, they notice the leaves, the blossoms, and the seeds; they know that no matter how temporary, life will go on.

Birth is the beginning of the spectrum of this life.

I received a call from a young woman not too long ago. Excitedly she said, "I went to the doctor today and he diagnosed me as pregnant." So there you have it, in the eye of the medical community pregnancy had become a disease and so it must be treated as a disease. I am appalled by the fact that this sacred time in the life of a living human being is now considered a disease.

Since the beginning of time, women have known how to have babies. The bodies of women have not forgotten how, but the conditions women are expected to abide by have changed nature's most precious offering.

A short time after I returned from Afghanistan, I was talking to a physician friend and was told that the elective Caesarian section rate in the state of Arizona, where I reside, was up to 37%. The normal rate is between 5% and 10%; these are the necessary procedures which save the lives of mothers and babies.

As I thought about this medical intervention I realized that the Afghani women were in trouble because they knew nothing about the physical aspect of birthing; our women do not realize that the many aspects of birthing, emotional, mental, spiritual, and even physical, are damaged when the natural process of birthing is interfered with.

Just picking a date on the calendar for convenience or some other arbitrary reason can impact both the baby and mother at the soul level. Fortunately, gynecologists across our country are beginning to realize that this needs to change and the number of C-sections has begun to come back down.

There may be times when a mother needs help with having her baby, and there is a time when a Caesarean section saves the life of mother and child. Intervention, however, is frequently not warranted or necessary and may be harmful.

Women, in my experience, deal quite well with pain, but we don't deal well with fear and abandonment. In the years when I was working with women who were birthing babies, I became aware that my job was to assist them. I was not the one who "delivered" the baby. I birthed six babies of my own, but my work with women in labor was to help them as they birthed their own babies.

Since pregnancy and birthing are the natural development of the human race, this magnificent, sacred life affirming process only requires that the one in attendance at the birth supports and assists the mother and the baby with love, knowledge and understanding. The process of birthing is an innate knowledge deep in each woman's soul and every birth is unique. A surgeon's knife is needed only when *absolutely necessary. As we have seen, when the practices of Caesarian sections escalate, we create more problems.*

We are exquisite and elegant beings, communicating through our senses with our mothers, in utero. These bonds of non-verbal communication are integral parts of how we develop to be who we are. Nature takes care of what nature has created.

When I returned from Afghanistan in 2005, I spoke of the conditions of women as they birthed their babies there. Because they didn't understand the anatomy or the physiology of pregnancy and delivery, they used severe external pressure in order to deliver the baby. This caused problems such as tears of the perineum, ruptured uterus, and ruptured bladders, leading to maternal death.

There are many other reasons why Afghani women have one of the highest rates of maternal death in the world. They, because they did not know any better, were damaging themselves on a physical level. We, on the other hand, don't know what we are doing to the incoming soul.

"Ovulation is a law of nature, and conception is a law of God." The body comprehends that it is only a channel, chosen for the expression of something sacred.

Conscious conception means that before the egg implants in the wall of the uterus, the mother has taken time and thought to prepare her body, mind and spirit to receive this amazing gift.

Wendy McCord Ph.D writes about being connected: "We must first understand that being connected is a basic human need, and a universal truth. We all began our life's journey in the state of connection with the great Oneness." Dr. McCord is an Old Lady who is devoting herself to the study of life. She sees this disconnect as the root and origin of human pain and suffering; the origin of our problems with self-esteem and love.

In her book' Earthbabies - Ancient Wisdom for Modern Times,' she says, "To the degree that a child was not intentionally conceived, or wanted, or finally accepted in the mother and father's heart, it will not feel connected. To the degree that it was wanted, and a place made in the mind and hearts of the parents, this child will know itself to be valuable and important. No other lesson in life can teach this so deeply. The time for this lesson is before conception and during womb time." Our connection and bond to our parents helps us feel love and enables us to give love. If parents do not have self-respect, it is hard for them to teach it to their children.

Dr. McCord explains the Empty Well that we all are as our life begins. We are a well that can be filled with love, poison, or simple indifference. It is in the manner by which we fill this empty well that the rest of our lives find definition.

Let us remember that a new birth is a beginning of a dance between a mother and the child. To dance well, we must be conscious of our dancing partner. Conscious birth begins this process. It is from this place that Dr. McCord believes that the survival of humanity and the human spirit will blossom. Waking up to what is being demanded of us is essential. We are the creators of the world we complain about.

It is an honor to be alive today. Information vital to the survival of the species and the earth is at our fingertips. Knowing that an honor is not bestowed without consideration, we must face the task in full consciousness. We are blessed to have had Old Ladies to pave the way for us, to hold with their roots the soil we walk on.

The whole of humanity has trouble facing matters of birth and death, afraid to face life on life's terms. Paying no attention to divine and natural laws, we are destroying ourselves.

In the field of obstetrics, when we arbitrarily choose a time for a baby to be born through elective C-section, we have no idea what we may be disrupting. In our arrogance, we have forgotten that each human being has a soul purpose, and each should be allowed to fulfill this purpose in her own timing.

When I was being born, my mother had a midwife and a doula in attendance. They were older experienced women in their field who were devoting the time it took for me to make my appearance. I am told I was a breach baby and the doula knew what to do.

Today, to offer continuous assistance to a mother and her baby, the use of electronic fetal monitoring devices have been introduced. "Human Hands Not Needed" could be written on these monitors.

C-Section babies are more apt to have difficulties with

suckling at their mother's breast and to make matters worse, mothers have been made to feel "old-fashioned" if their breast is used by their baby for nourishing, body and soul.

Children born of C-sections do not get a chance to enter the birth canal; when their passage into the world does not follow the natural pattern, they can have lifelong problems. The rhythmic contractions of birthing help to empty the baby's lungs of the amniotic fluid, so the first breath is clear. Caesarian babies are more apt to have respiratory problems. After C-sections mothers often suffer pelvic pain, bowel blockages, bladder and uterine infections, ectopic pregnancies, and uterine rupture. It is, after all, major abdominal surgery. Malpractice insurances call this natural occurrence a procedure.

Chapter 34
Father Time, Mother Nature

Harry lived to be 104 years of age. Not all of my patients reach that benchmark. He came to consult with me and we had a conversation. Meet my friend Harry, He will not mind if you listen in.

"How are you Harry?'

"Doing just fine, Father Time , Mother Nature, they take care of me."

His spirit was fresh and resilient, and he was able to deal with each of life's issues he faced without complaining or feeling sorry for himself. He wore age as a beautiful cloak, and learned to meet the needs of the condition.

When she was in her late seventies, Harry's wife developed a hernia. She needed to have it repaired. Her English was highly accented and she told me that she was not afraid have this "hornia'" repaired because she had great "fate.'" That was good. But her faith did not stop her from saying 'Gladys, I' m a fatalist.' It was after her death that Harry came to visit me; it had been twelve years since his wife had died and he was still vibrant; he too had 'great fate.'

Grand Mother Moon told me, 'we rationalize instead of

letting our Mother and Father take care us.' So much wisdom all around us; so many old people, men and of course Old Ladies, have stories to bring us to points of acceptance and gratitude.

My 89 year old friend lives in a retirement home. A nice place and there he has a small room, set up with the things he needs. This is a person who traveled many countries. He had owned precious art and other objects; he had been surrounded with the best of everything, but now things had changed and his memory was going, life was confusing. When I visited him, he told me how happy he was in this one room. "There is even that magic box." He walked to the thermostat and said, "See, it's magic. It's hot in the room right now but if I push this lever down, it cools off; if I get too cool, I push the lever up. It's a magic box." I was so delighted with his comment. The ability to turn a simple thermostat into a magic box that takes care of your environment is pure genius, and magical too. In our world today, the economy is shifting and many of us are having a hard time adjusting to what we have lost, all that we have to do without. Our challenge is to reframe our lives and start appreciating what we do have.

To focus on what is present in life permits me full interaction with what is real, what is necessary, what is magical. When I was young I had no time for gratitude; I was engaged in the matters of youth. Now with some memories, I can even have gratitude.

As children in India my siblings and I learned to entertain ourselves; we took what was available to us for whatever we were imagining or working with. My sister and I learned to knit.

My knitting needles were made of wire sharpened . Any piece of yarn or wool that we found became a ball of yarn. We made clothing for our dolls. We were lucky our Ayah had shown us the basic knitting stitches and from there we improved and learned how to adjust those stitches to make the clothes our dolls needed.

When life's circumstances cause us to cut back to our basic needs, we often find ourselves happier and more content, as we can draw from the reservoir of our life's experience to help us through hard times.

We can moan and groan about the hardships that come our way, or we can dwell in gratitude. This action moves us out of fear, and into the flow of life. This is how Father Time and Mother Nature take care of us.

And Oh! What We Can Learn From The Little Ones.

When my youngest grandson was about four, he said to me,"I think the meanest thing that anybody could do is to take away all of the teddy bears and blankies." And then he said. "Couldn't we send teddy bears and blankies to Iraq instead of bombs?"

I thought oh, how wonderful out of the minds of babes – teddy bears and blankies, which were his precious things, were what he wanted to share with children who didn't have them in places of the world that he had heard of.

At another time we were sitting around my dining room table playing the game, "I spy with my little eye something that's green or blue or whatever" and after a little while one of the other children gave up. Taylor looked at me proudly and he said, "I never give up." So we played a little while longer and some one else gave up, and Taylor said, "I never give up." So we played a little while longer and all of a sudden Taylor jumped down off of the chair, ran around, ran around the living room, came back in, climbed up on the chair, looked at me and said, "Sometimes I take a rest, but I never give up."

And I thought, " what a beautiful lesson to teach me, Taylor." The idea is that there are times in our lives when we simply don't have the energy or the will to keep on going, but we don't give up. We just say, "I'm going to take a rest."

This is particularly helpful when a person has a chronic illness and has tried everything. They've worked and worked and have not been able to get well, and they've just gotten tired of keeping on, keeping on. Then, maybe they get invited to a birthday party and they eat a piece of cake and realize, "I shouldn't have done that", and they think they have blown the whole thing and they give up. If only, instead of giving up, they could say to their bodies, "Oh, my, I took a rest but I don't give up." and continue on the path that allows them a rest time.

If you think about it, every time you climb a flight of stairs after a few stairs there is a resting place, a landing where you rest and then you go on. That is part of life. That is the way of facing things as they come to us in our lives.

Chapter 35
Growth and Change

My garden is a sort of encyclopedia; it contains a vocabulary which I sometimes understand has medicinal plants to help me heal. The rains of spring had fallen; the sky was blue, my mind was filled with excitement and anticipation. I was envisioning the fruits; from the seeds I held in my hand. I had grown enough now to know how to plant.

I wanted a patch of dirt, a very small piece of the earth, to produce what the best of the seeds had to offer me. The idea that nature would produce only what was needed in my garden was already part of what I experienced, I knew the natural world would do its best, and struggle to grow and give me something strong and different from the seeds held tight in my hand.

From prior experiences, I knew not all my seeds would make it. As my thoughts ran wild, I thought of the Old Lady who talked to me about "the way" I was beginning to understand. Biology had taught me my seeds would enter a different reality, they would establish roots. Their stems would grow and one day present me with their bounty.

Nature, being shaped by the will to survive, would know what to do. I would do my part the best way I knew how, and from a seed a completely different life form would come forth, a miracle would happen.

I could not help but think we are all in a constant state of transition. To let this happen, we sometimes need to let go of the past.

The embryo has to be willing to let go of old patterns and develop new ones. If, at any place along the path, it decides to keep the old and not receive the new, it dies. In order to grow and develop into a human, it has to constantly, on a molecular level, be willing to change to live. So often in life I have felt I did not want to change; nor did I want anything around me to change. An Old Lady suggested that at all levels, be they physical, mental or spiritual. changes must take place in order to have growth.

There comes the time for the baby to be born. There must be a letting go of the comfort and security of the womb to come out into the world where it will have to breathe and eat and get rid of its waste on its own. No longer can the mother do this for her. For the rest of her life, she will have to be willing to give and to receive on all levels, physical, mental and spiritual.

Only as she is willing to do this, will she continue to grow, perhaps not taller or wider, new cells are constantly being formed and destroyed. Breathing in and out, food in and out, muscles contracting and relaxing, this is the way of life.

Everything changes, and when all this stops, we die. Then we have to give up the physical so that the soul can continue its journey. As the life force travels from the roots up the trunk, it takes the nutrients and transforms them into living juices so that the tree can continue to grow.

I do not remember my journey from the womb to this world. Now older and wiser, I question, will I remember the journey from life to life? I trust, since I now have life, I must give it my best in order to establish strong roots, grow strong limbs, and struggle with the demands of life itself. This too is the way. I may leave behind something of value to some, but in the end, this is an individual journey for each of us. What a privilege this process is!

The Chinese say pain comes from blocked Chi.

When we try to hang on to something physical that no longer serves its purpose, we create a block, and this results in physical pain.

On an emotional level, if we try to hang on to the love of a person who has already moved on, the pain is that of a broken heart.

On the mental level, if we have concepts, ideologies, or theologies that no longer serve us as our knowledge has grown and our understanding has evolved, then the mental conflict can cause severe distress.

On the spiritual level, if we try to hang on to our experience of God from the past when we have had experiences of a living, loving God; and then something happens that makes us feel separated from God and our very living source, this can become the dark night of the soul.

We are then blocked, and the block can only be relieved as we move through it, into the light. We need to let go of the old that has become dark. When it was right for us, it was light, but as we moved through it become dark, and became our shadow.

The very act of being demands that we understand and accept change and flexibility. Like waves at sea, this is a process elegantly seen within life itself. The more we become attached to feelings, hang on to objects and results, the more we suffer from the difficulties and fears that render us prisoners.

Some of the problems within today's society may also come from the fact that there are too many demands on the family. The time when within the working model of a home every person held a particular role, seems to have changed. The roles were respected for what they were and every player knew his place.

When we watch a football game, soccer, baseball or other game where teamwork is necessary, we notice every player having a role. Perhaps the societal disconnect happens because the family roles are changing, and our job is to adjust to the change.

In the classroom, children and teachers are faced with the changing times. We have tools that have never been available to us before, and children who understand how to use them. This can be very disrupting in the classroom. We don't want creative children disrupting the classroom, so we medicate them to keep them in line. We overwork our teachers, so they don't have the time and patience to help direct this energy; furthermore, we overcrowd the classrooms.

The great minds of our youth are either addicted or medicated, so they have trouble allowing themselves to get truly zealous about any cause. I heard many years ago that the way wars were won in the Middle East, in ancient times, was that one country would get the soldiers of the enemy hooked on Hashish. They then had no fight left in them, and the country was taken over. Their Chi was blocked.

As individuals, it is only as we look honestly at difficult places and our shadow side that we can feel the love and joy of our true nature. Peace only comes from dealing with conflict in an open, natural way, and being willing to look at all sides and deal rationally with the conflict. The conflict is not the problem it is our choice to deal with it and resolve the issues, or try to avoid them so then they become blocked and growth is stopped.

Dr. Gladys often says, "It's a privilege to be alive today." It is indeed an honor to be alive today. Information vital to the survival of the species and the earth is at our fingertips. Knowing that an honor is not bestowed without due consideration, we must face the task in full consciousness.

How lucky we are to have had Old Ladies to pave the way for us, to hold with their roots the soil we walk on. They teach us about creation and about birth and about death. These lessons are not lost, in our rushing world, we are given choices for how we will deal with the conflict.

Jesus said, "I came to give you life, and that more abundantly." The only way we can have an abundant life is by allowing ourselves to live, not shy away from life, or try to sleep through it.

We can allow children to get hot and sweaty and dirty so they can feel how great a shower feels, let them participate in other people's losses and hunger so they can know how blessed they are, and let them feel their own pain and loss and help them face it and grow through it. We fail to understand that growth is something that over and over again comes from active participation in the life process, and it can be painful.

With children, if some medication is needed, that can often be okay, but it is not the first thing to go for. We help them take responsibility for their own healing. We can't digest their food for them; we can't digest their life experiences for them; it is something they have to do for themselves.

We are individually responsible for the health of each cell in our body. The nourishment we give them on all levels, body, mind and spirit, is up to each one of us. We are individually responsible for getting nutrients to the cells and for removing wastes from them. No one else can do it for us. Even with a blood transfusion, we individually have to get those red cells where they need to go - no one else can do that for us.

It is in this spirit that I see a brotherhood and solidarity, between each cell in our body. Since we represent only a small part of a larger body, it is also my understanding that we should make efforts to use this same type of brotherhood toward other members of the community of mankind.

Looking at our tree of life, I know the tree does not begin at the trunk, nor do the branches blossom until ready. The seasons determine the order by which the tree will provide us some fruits. We must look to the roots to find the answer we are searching for.

Conscious conception means that before the egg implants in the wall of the uterus the mother has taken time and thought to prepare her body, mind and spirit to receive this amazing gift.

We take the time to prepare a meal so we can enjoy the

taste. We cultivate and prepare the soil before we plant a garden. Yet, too often we don't take the time to prepare ourselves for pregnancy. Birth and death are the two things we all have in common. To live these two stages of our life's passages, we should prepare ourselves physically, mentally and spiritually. This has been true for hundreds of years.

The World Needs Old Ladies

Chapter 36
To Live Until We Die

Numerous rings can be found within the trunk in our tree of life. The Old Ladies left us the rings of wisdom and consciousness. Each ring tells the story of a year in a life. They are the keepers of the stories left to us by the Old Ladies. There is organization and divine order, and there is also a time when the relationship between each can be examined.

In the organized way of writing this book with Dr. Gladys we each took on a journey neither had planned. Knowing at one level or another that life travels where we had not yet been, we followed our individual sense of direction. We are after all individuals with different life experiences. Different by heritage, country of origin, spiritual guidance and religion makes us an unlikely pair. Yet, at another level, we are both very much alike, even if we express our thoughts with a different voice.

When Dr. Gladys called me one day and began a long sentence without a pause, I heard, "I think you need to write the next chapter without my input. You are experiencing an approach to the end of a life close to you, one you love and admire."

Up to that moment, my expericnce of understanding, accepting and digesting matters of life and death had been singular and personal. I love life and am passionate about many issues and yet I am a singular individual. My experiences with issues of end of life could only be the result of the sum total of who I become on a daily basis.

This book began with a circle and at its roots we understood its all-encompassing embrace to the earth, to all that it represents, and all that we are. Only the trunk of our tree of life could contain the wisdom, grown from deep roots. While both our roots were deep and firmly planted, I was not sure I had the tools necessary to handle what had been asked of me.

It is not typical to pay attention to the expression of a human life in a tree trunk. We pay very little attention to the value of the bark, encircling the acquired wisdom of our metaphor. It is when we look up at the branches, the leaves, the blossoms and the fruits that we approach an understanding of what life might mean to each of us.

All things having a beginning must also come to an end, including the circle of life itself. There is a mundane, literary understanding to this statement. Dr. Gladys wanted to know what the core of my journey was. She could have written this last chapter because, like me, she knows what it brings to the table.

It is within this circle that I continue what I have come to observe as perhaps the greatest moments of my life. To write this ending chapter I must expose myself to you, the reader. I must be close and personal with people I do not know. I must allow you to know what I feel. I learned that matters of life and death are indeed personal, yet they too come with lessons to share and lessons to learn.

It was not too long ago when my husband was told of a series of chronic ailments that would take his life. Perhaps I came to face my own mortality. We all know, intimately or not, that we are born to die; yet at the doors of death we feel pain and anger at the fact that we have not yet finished our journey. It is within this process that I came to understand the cliché that life is precious.

With this understanding, I want to talk about the relationship of each partner within the connection one human being can have with another.

When we are young, we take the word relationship and think it is associated to sex. When we have children we think of an association with ownership. Our hearts get broken, they feel trepidation, and they feel pain and great joy. We do not think about matters relating to the end of life.

I have come to realize these emotions are sensations we all can and probably will all experience. Yet it is in witnessing the lurking of death at the door that I have come to appreciate living fully.

Most of us come from societies where no one dares talk of death in an open manner. "He or she will die, but I am eternal", seems to be the attitude. Or if we do not talk about "it" we are safe, "it" will not happen.

Having spent many Tuesday evenings with Dr. Gladys and among other powerful women I woke up to myself. Most times, people that are around us do not know how they impact our lives.

I do not claim to understand all the material we have reviewed, talked about or even experienced. I have found, because of these discussions, I have grown to be a stronger better-balanced human being. I do not understand all there is to life but I am confident that one can be honest with one's "self" without fear or guilt. Be assured however, that fear, guilt and various degrees of anger are usually behind a door, much like an old broom placed there and ready to be used.

A good friend wanted to know what kind of honesty I was talking about. The answer to this can only be mine, because I cannot tell with certainly what can and cannot work for anyone else.

Working closely with Dr. Gladys, I noted her intimate understanding of birth and what it meant to the universe each time. I also noted her understanding of end of life. Traveling the road of life, a day at a time, and one step at a time, one moment after the other, I can now say to my husband, "When you die, I will…" The first time we ventured in such a dialogue, there were moments that were tense and painful. After all, we both come from societies where no one talks of death until it is too late. Now, steady on our feet, we can even joke and say, "How do you know you will not die before I do?" Most of all, we can appreciate that we are fully alive, whatever the conditions of that life.

We both arrived at the conclusion, at least for ourselves, when we are afraid to speak about the end of our life, we are also afraid to live our lives fully. When we are afraid, we are controlled by circumstances and we become victims.

Once we found this understanding, it seems other doors opened to our awareness. We can plan the unpleasant tasks that lie ahead in a natural way. We can plan vacations the way we always did, now knowing that the plan may have to change. We remember planning an outing and at the last moment changing our mind.

There was a time when these changes were taken lightly. Nothing has changed and our lives continue to be the teacher we need. We are engaged in matters of being alive while in the process of dying. It was always like that but we simply did not stop to recognize the reality of impermanence.

The only difference I can see is that we are now aware that life is not a permanent station, and that it is precious.

Life takes practice and within this practice experiences are presented to grow with and to grow from. The growing pains of my youth are different today. My husband experiences parallel mine; he is after all only human.

In our humanness, we communicate the feelings we have. These exchanges of feelings and information take equal and sometimes greater practice because one must first examine what is going on way inside. We waver sometimes, we weaken at other times, we are afraid at times of the unknown, but most of the time we are joyous to be able to experience our lives in a state of gratitude.

As Dr. Gladys says often, "Isn't great to be alive today? " It is in this process that I have learned to be fully conscious, and to fully awaken to life. Something grand happens to the spirit when one becomes conscious and honest. One becomes aware of the gift of life.

I will sorely miss the interactions with my husband because

we have grown and worked toward being balanced people, aware of our demise. We also have and continue to grow a bond between us that not all people experience. It is in this knowledge that we can learn to become better humans.

I will miss our great conversations, and I will miss our discussions about things we see differently, or the ones we understand within our core. I will miss his laughter, his touch, and his affection.

I will not miss knowing my capacity to love, there will be no guilt, and yet a great void will envelop me I am sure.

Our engagement is one of bliss because we are after all both alive today. There is good feeling about the expression of life even as it is unfolding to what it was predisposed to do.

I know in my life I received a gift to be appreciated and to learn from, I have memories to be cherished, and perhaps nothing more is needed.

Should I die before my husband does, he will feel the things I know to be true.

Chapter 37
Old Mother Hubbard's Cupboard

A book with Dr. Gladys, or because of Dr. Gladys, could not end without some remedies. Each one of us can look back on our lives and remember something that some one told us which was considered an old outdated cure. Perhaps this is the time to look at it again and remember where this information came from. An Old Lady may have known something which was laughed at and it was thrown away. Families and cultures have much which is wise and has not been studied.

I still laugh when I recall her telling us what her children would have inscribed on her headstone: "Here she lies - in spite of castor oil"

The headstone part may be a joke, but the castor oil part is not. Palma Christi is a name they gave this oil. Palma is the palm, Christi is the Christ. If any of you have seen the leaf of the castor plant, you will note the leaf has five 'fingers'.

We touched on the virtue of this oil, which not only stays on top of your skin, but also penetrates the skin. Your lymphatic system accepts it and makes good use of it.

A castor oil pack is helpful for chronic indigestion. Used with heat over the liver area for one to one-and-a-half hours, it stimulates the peristalsis in the bowel, and activates the digestive enzymes. If, however, you are having acute abdominal pain, it is important first of all that you see a doctor, second, that you do not use heat. The castor oil pack will help without heat. When there is acute abdominal pain, heat is contraindicated.

When I returned home from the hospital after my ruptured esophagus, I was told I would to have only a liquid diet. Being a vegetarian that did not seem difficult or impossible. I began putting castor oil on my throat. The only inconvenience was the fact that castor oil is a heavy oil and it oiled my top sheet. I did learn to put a cloth between my well-saturated throat and the sheet. I am here to tell you that today I eat whatever ever I want.

Dr. Gladys offered me an explanation about castor oil; she talked about balance and belief in a therapy that helped the 'physician within' do the work that it needed to do.

Balance between the kidney and the liver is essential; coordination between the sympathetic and the parasympathetic nervous system is also necessary. Castor oil packs help promote this coordination. In Chinese medicine they say that pain and sickness comes from the chi energy being blocked; acupuncture allows the flow of the energy. Castor oil assists the lymphatic flow.

Family and friends of Dr. Gladys all know about Castor Oil Packs. This would be an unfinished work if I did not write down how to prepare one.

Instructions for Use:

Fold a piece of wool flannel, (cotton flannel is all right if wool is not available or there is an allergy to wool) so it is 2 – 4 layers thick and measures about 10" x 12". Saturate with castor oil, (for general detoxification purposes apply the pack over the liver area).

Then cover the pack with a piece of plastic (Saran wrap or a garbage bag will do). Place a heating pad on top of that, set to the low temperature. Do not make it too hot. A hot water bottle can also be used.

Then wrap a towel, folded length-wise around the entire area and fasten it with safety pins. The heating pad should remain in place for 1 hour only. The pack itself can be worn all night without heat.

The skin can be cleaned after the treatment by using soda water (to a quart of water, add two teaspoons of baking soda).

Keep the flannel pack in a plastic container for future use. It is possible to use the same pack for different problems and need not be discarded after one application. Typically, you can use your same pack for a number of injuries, but when dealing with a very toxic condition, it would be best to throw the pack away when the condition is healed.

DO NOT ATTEMPT TO DRYCLEAN YOUR PACK – this just adds unwanted chemicals.

As I age gracefully, I use castor oil packs as often as Dr. Gladys suggests for various aches and pains.

Volumes have been written about Palma Christi; people

familiar with holistic medicine, or living medicine, use this oil as a first line of defense. Gladys' many years working with the ARE (Association for Research & Enlightenment), founded by the family of Edgar Cayce, allowed her to study the value of many remedies, including castor oil packs, on her patients.

This book will not be complete without a few other remedies and good advice.

Most families have their own cupboard full of remedies which they can use.

A patient with sinus infection was helped by not eating chocolate. Another gave up milk products. Unfortunately, the ice cream lover also had to give that up. As I think of sinus I must add sugar to my list, it is a major causative factor in any infection, sinus infection included. There are times when sinus congestion is brought on because of withheld tears.

When these remedies do not alleviate or treat the problem, medical help may be needed. An antibiotic may be necessary especially if there is a fever accompanying the sinus problems. Please always remember to eat live yogurt or take acidophilus when taking antibiotics. Yeast infections are not fun.

I suffer from sinus congestions because my sinuses do not drain properly when I am in a prone position.

With congestions, she recommends the use of Glyco-Thymoline packs, (available over the counter at some drugstores). The pack should cover the forehead. Cover the pack with plastic and then a heating pad, set on low for about 20 to 30 minutes.

Imagine, more than once, I had my castor oil pack on my

neck, my Glyco-Thymoline pack on my face — my husband was kind enough to take no photos. He did not even complain when my two tennis balls were also part of my loving head. That too was to help my sinus congestion. Pressure points on the back of the neck at the base of the skull, where the head bone meets the neck bone, are frequently tender when a person has sinus congestion. These points are also acupuncture points. If a person applies deep pressure in this area, it can help with sinus pain and helps the sinuses drain. One way of applying this pressure is to use two tennis balls tied close enough together in a sock so that is causes pressure on these points when a person rests her head back against the sock.

I have not had a cold since I met Dr. Gladys. It is not that I am not exposed to germs, but I knock them out the minute I feel a tingle in my throat. 3 to 6 thousand milligrams of Vitamin C and lots of water, no ice please, and two things happen: my body gets cleansed and germs decide it is OK to be flushed out of my system. Of course, Castor Oil rubbed on my chest acts like a back up army.

There was a time when almost nothing was known about nutrition. Sadly our medical doctors receive very little information about this in the course of their studies. We also did not know the effect of emotional stresses, or our way of thinking, having an effect on our joints, actually our entire body. We now know these things, and we also know that plenty of exercise, drinking lots of water, helps our joints.

The role of glucosamine and chondroitin has come to play an important part in the health of our joints. These two products are helpful in keeping the cartilage of our joints healthy and in helping to rebuild them. After taking these products for a period of time, I progressively feel my joints working better.

Having found her taste for food in India, Dr. Gladys has a diet filled with curries, cinnamon, turmeric and spices.

I have found cherries when in season, reduce pain and inflammation, much like one of the NSAID drugs we take when we have a headache.

Sweet potatoes have lots of fiber, and we all need fibers to keep us clean.

When I was young, whenever I had a cold or the flu, my mother made a very strong infusion of elderberry, and I was to drink cups of this very hot tea with plenty of honey. I have since learned that this ancient remedy contains flavonoids, which compare well with what we buy at the drugstore, Timaflu. As an adult, I do not get the flu, but I do use elderberry.

I grew up in a variety of islands and when people took too many aspirins their stomach often developed ulcers. They were given coconut milk or coconut water, both delightful. I faked many stomach ailments just to get more Coconut milk.

The Old Ladies from some islands gave people who according to them ate the wrong foods, extract of the kiwi fruit along with hawthorn, they make a potion out of the two, and it is taken by the tablespoonful. There is now evidence that the combination of the two lowers cholesterol.

In the Middle East, an infusion with honey, cinnamon and lemon juice first thing in the morning seems to help those with cholesterol problems.

My friend with a tendency to develop kidney stones has been drinking lemonade. He makes strong lemonades with real lemons, and everyday has a glass. No kidney stones have made any appearance in over a decade.

My Jamaican friend told me that in "traditional Jamaican medicine" unripe papaya is used on chronic skin ulcers. They have been doing so since they discovered this wonderful fruit.

Aloe vera has been used for centuries for many skin conditions, including burns. I know some people have cured their stomach ulcers with aloe water. This plant, I am convinced, helped in the healing my esophagus. The juice from the plant, did not taste good; I did not like its slimy appearance. But sometimes the doctor within speaks to us. I heard her say "do you really want to get well?"

Aloe water can be made by taking a large aloe frond from the plant – peeling the heavy green skin off, using just the inner part - place it in the pitcher and fill the pitcher with water. All of the water you drink is from that pitcher. As you take a glass of water out, you replace it with a fresh glass of water.

My husband, with all his cardiac problems, gets a drink every day that contains every berry I can get my hands on. Strawberries, being the primary component of this drink, seem to relax the lining of the blood vessels, thus his blood pressure is reduced.

Ananas is the fruit I know, the one you call pineapple, and it contains bromelain. I know it is effective for bruises, sprains, strains, because it reduces swelling. In my family, we ate pineapple as many people eat apples. My mother, her grandmother, and the other Old Ladies before them used this fruit for indigestion, a supply of vitamin C, and also because it made their skin look good.

Ancient Greek physicians used vinegar for relief from arthritis. Some use it to help with heartburn. Vinegar can be used to treat ear infections and also yeast infections. I clean my windows with it, and also my skin.

When using vinegar, please find raw, fermented, unfiltered, apple cider vinegar. You also do not want it to be pasteurized. It restores our natural PH balance. Our blood supply needs to be alkaline not acidic. Many studies have proven that cancer cells do not grow in alkaline solutions. A more alkaline PH can also be accomplished by taking half a teaspoonful of baking soda in half a glass of water at bed time.

I use other remedies also, and have told others about beef juice.

BEEF JUICE

Beef juice is not a broth, but a juice extracted from the beef through the process of heat. It is prepared as follows:

Take about one pound of round steak. Cut off the fat, leaving the muscles and pieces of tendon, then cut it up into very small pieces. Put the pieces into a glass jar without water in it. The jar should be covered but not tightly. Then put the jar into a pan with water in it, the water coming about ½ to ¾ of the way toward the top of the jar. Put a cloth at the bottom of the pan to prevent the jar from cracking. Let the water simmer for 2 hours.

Then strain the juice, which has accumulated in the jar, as

the meat will then be worthless. Place the juice in a refrigerator, but never keep it longer than 3 days. It should be taken 2 to 3 times a day, but not more than a tablespoon at a time and this should be sipped very slowly taking perhaps 5 to 10 minutes. This is important because the digestion starts in the mouth, and the amino acids are taken into the blood stream, thus bypassing the other digestive juices.

Beef Juice is very helpful specially when a malnourished person needs additional protein.

Did you know that before we had antibiotics, potatoes were used to draw out the pus from boils?

POTATO POULTICE

This is an ancient remedy, found perhaps as part of every country's folk medicine, especially where potatoes are grown. Its value lies we know in the active enzymes that are released when the potato is scraped to make the poultice, breaking down the cells of the tuber. It can be used as therapy for the eyes.

To make a potato poultice, take a piece of white cloth large enough to cover the eye adequately and place it on a flat surface. Then take a raw "old Irish" potato, the kind usually used for baking, and wash it well, leaving the skin on.

Then, using a paring knife, start scraping the potato onto the cloth. Don't pare it, but scrape it. You will gradually scrape off a quantity of mush-like material. When a third to a half of the potato is used, this will probably be sufficient.

Shape the material into two portions one for each eye and put it on the cloth, slip your hands under the cloth and carefully (after closing your eyes) lay the poultice directly over the eyes. Leave it in place for 20 to 30 minutes; after removing the poultice, wash off the dried residue with hot water. This can be used twice a week, the frequency depends on the condition being treated.

I think the greatest remedy I received from Dr. Gladys came in the form of a prescription and it said: Rest. I was even able to read her handwriting.

Then, of course, there is grandmother medicine.

I have found that when life makes demands, I cannot always immediately respond. The answers searched for, are seldom far from us. Sometimes the answer comes from a small child one who wrote:

"What is a Grandmother", written in 1991, by a 3rd Grader:

"A grandmother is a lady who has no children of her own. She likes other people's little girls. A grandfather is a man grandmother. He goes for walks with the boys and they talk about fishing, and tractors, and things like that. Grandmothers don't have to do anything but be there. They're so old they shouldn't play hard or run. It is enough if they take us to the market where the pretend horse is, and have lots of dimes ready.

They take us for walks and slow down for passing things like pretty leaves or caterpillars. They never say "Hurry up".

Usually they are fat, but not too fat to tie your shoes. They wear glasses. They do not have to be smart, only answer questions like why dogs hate cats, and how come God isn't married. They read to us, they don't skip words; or mind if it is the same story time and time again.Everybody should try to have one, especially if they don't have a television, because grandmothers are the only grown-ups who have time."

These, ofcourse, are old fashoned grandmothers who may be hard to find now.

In this book, both Dr. Gladys and I took the time to show you that we are Old Ladies, and grandmothers, too. Like the Grandmother above, we did not do anything but explore what we found growing in and around our individual trees, things like old copper pennies.

An ant bit my daughter-in-law, and it was very painful. We didn't have anything with us except our purses, and I remembered that I had been able to help someone in a similar situation in the past. So I got a copper penny out of my purse and just placed it on the bite. We sat down to rest, and within 20 minutes the pain was gone and the swelling receded.

Carry a copper penny with you - you never know when you might need it. It might remind you of an Old Lady who told you stories.

And here is a new/old use for Aspirin.

A doctor friend of mine told me a really good story. He was a medical doctor in Santa Barbara, California, and loved to go deep-sea fishing. On one of these trips with his wife and friends, they hit a bad storm. He became so seasick that he was lying on the deck of the ship, throwing up.

His wife was sympathetic for a while but finally said, "You really should try what your patient told you. I know it doesn't make any sense, but here is an aspirin and a bandaid. Tape it in to your bellybutton,"

He was willing to do anything so he taped it in and finished the trip standing and fishing.

I have used this remedy many times, on many trips and with many people, even on a two year old and it has worked. I have many stories to tell about it and still don't know how it works except that it works. I think it has something to do with the energy pathways crossing at the navel.

Note: Coated Aspirin does not work.

It was a week after I heard this story that a friend of mine was going on a cruise, her first cruise. When she felt the seasickness coming on she looked for an Aspirin and found she had none. She was getting sicker by the minute.

She knocked on the door of the cabin next to hers and asked the gentleman who answered the door if he had an Aspirin. He did but was curious, "Most people take two Aspirin; I could spare a second one." My friend explained that it was for her bellybutton. Of course the puzzled man wanted to know more.

I am told that within two days everyone on board knew the cure for motion sickness, one Aspirin and one bandaid.

It is important to understand that these suggestions are not given as prescriptions.

They are being shared with you, from two Old Ladies, as part of our history in the hope that you may find some thing in your lives which may have been concidered an 'old wives tale,'but it had worked for your family. It might be an onion poltice for congestion, or soup made from soup bones for stronger bones. Lets not discard the old concepts, just because they are old. It is possible that science may catch up with the old thoughts and find value in them.

Chapter 38
Mother Goose

This book is a gathering of thoughts, stories, therapies, and lifetimes.

Because we needed to have some sort of framework on which we could present this material, we chose The Tree Of Life. We have loosely strung together the material to fit our ideas of where things should go. You, dear reader, may or may not see the reason for the positioning of these concepts, or even the concepts themselves, but that is okay. It makes sense to us, and we are Old Ladies.

Life's experiences shift things around; what is properly placed at one time may be way out of place at another. That is the way life is.

Take and use what you can; put the rest up on a shelf. The time may come when it fits into your life, and then it will make sense. A half baked pie tastes awful, but a pie, given the right amount of time to bake thoroughly, is a joy.

We Old Ladies are well baked; we have lived through the hottest of times and the coldest - and we are still here. Please do not take what we have to say lightly.

During the time when I was trying to make some sense out

of our national healthcare program, I finally remembered three Nursery Rhymes that clarified the picture for me.

1st

>*There was an old woman*
>*Who lived in a shoe,*
>*She had so many children*
>*She didn't know what to do.*
>*She gave them some milk*
>*Without any bread*
>*And whipped them soundly*
>*And put them to bed.*

This poor old woman is our worn out old healthcare system She is old and tired and stuck in one shoe. A person can't go anywhere in one shoe.

Our healthcare is stuck in the belief that our healing work is to cure diseases, not to heal people. This model cannot go anywhere.

She has so many children she doesn't know what to do. The diseases are her children. When we are treating diseases, there is no end to it. Diseases create more diseases, as do many of the therapies we use to try to get rid of them.

She gives them some milk without any bread, and whips them soundly, and puts them to bed. The only thing she knows to do is to silence them.

This, to me as a physician for 66 years, means; to take care of the symptoms. Milk without any bread is just a temporary quieter. It does not work too well, so she whips them soundly and puts them to bed. We seem to think that if we are aggressive enough in our treatment of a disease, we can really make it stop bothering us. Now we have cured the disease? Unfortunately the children do wake up, so we are still stuck.

This old paradigm will not work; but there is hope, because we have another nursery rhyme.

2nd

> Mary had a little lamb
> Whose fleece was white as snow
> And every place that Mary went
> That lamb was sure to go.
> It followed her to school one day
> Which was against the rule.
> It made the children laugh and play
> To see a lamb at school.

There we have a real person, not an accumulation of diseases; and she even has a name. Mary has a little lamb, which can represent the Physician Within, or her own healing power. This healing power is pure energy, 'white as snow'.

Mary can't go anywhere with out her lamb. As long as we are alive, this healing energy is with us. Surgeons can repair our damaged tissues, but it is this energy that heals the wound.

It followed her to school one day, which was against the rule. The school of life has its own rules, which focus on diseases, not people. This type of healing is not welcome.

However, Mary is smart, and she gets around those rules, which makes every one happy.

This is the way Living Medicine works, and now the

3rd

Humpty Dumpty sat on a wall
Humpty Dumpty had a great fall
All the king's horses
And all the king's men
Couldn't put Humpty Dumpty
Together again.

Humpty Dumpty could represent our medical healthcare system, which has been on a wall, separated from the people it needs to work with. The Ivory Tower where decisions are made, is represented by his shell.

But life has been progressing, and within that shell real life has been growing. This could be the energy of the people, who are taking back their own healing power, and rocking the egg until it falls off of the wall.

Our National Healthcare Reform could be that little chick that comes out of the egg, and if it is, it really needs to be cared for, and helped to grow, into the system desperately needed for our people.

All the king's horses and all the kings men, to me seems to represent the number of presidents who have been trying to improve this System.

But I, a 92-year old lady doctor, can help.

They can never fix it as long as they think healing comes from the out side. However, life moves and grows within it; it will break its own shell and be set free. Our job now is to figure out what this chick needs to help it grow into the eagle it can become. One day, after I began to understand what these rhymes could mean, I was talking to a couple I had just met. They were doing documentary films and had just come to Phoenix. As I was going on and on about these three rhymes, Susan's eyes got bigger and bigger. When I stopped to take a breath, she said," Mother Goose was my relative eight generations ago. Her maiden name was Elizabeth Foster, and she married a man named Isaac Goose".

Now my mouth dropped open and my eyes popped wide open. I never thought Mother Goose was a real person, yet here was Susan, sitting there telling me she was a real person. She said her sister even owned a chair that had belonged to Mother Goose.

The way I remember the rest of the story is that, for much of her life, Susan had known about her relationship with Mother Goose, but had never thought whether the rhymes meant anything to people. They were words that rhymed, which children learned.

The family story was that Mother Goose married a widower who had 10 children, and then they had 6 of their own. So she truly was "An old woman, who had so many children she didn't know what to do."

The story goes on to say that all of her family and friends loved her, but weren't sure what to make of her rhymes. Apparently, while she was going about her household duties she would make up rhymes which helped her cope with her life.

Since she remembered them, she could repeat them.

She had a son-in law named Thomas Fleet, a printer, who one day realized the gift in her songs. He decided to start writing them down, and had great fun drawing pictures to go with them. When he had put them all together, he made them into a book, and sold quite a few. People loved them, and the rest is history.

So there you have it, Dear Readers.

Whether you read this chapter first or last, this is the story of life from two Old Ladies. They, like the Mother Goose from all nations, have messages to share with you.

Nursery rhymes may sound like empty rhyming words. However, if you read and listen with an open heart, you will find, at unexpected times in your life, words that begin to make your life easier, or help your life make more sense.

The things we have to say come from our hearts to yours . Just as Mother Goose's words helped her with the day-by-day chores, and have lightened the load of thousands of people in ways they did not know, may our thoughts help you, as they have helped us.

*So, in the words of my dear friend Dr. Alyce Green, when she was far along the path into Alzheimer's disease, as she looked into my eyes, " I don't know who you are, but I know I love you." It is, after all, the path of love that brings us all togethe*r.

Epilogue

After the manuscript of this book went to the type setter we came across some research validating that The World Needs Old Ladies.

According to Kristen Hawkes, an anthropologist at the University of Utah, who proposed the 'grandmother hypothesis', which states, "Grandmothering was the initial step toward making us who we are." Her theory explains menopause and the under-appreciated evolutionary value of grandmothering which helped us develop "a whole array of social capacities that are then the foundation for the evolution of other distinctly human traits, including pair bonding, bigger brains, learning new skills and our tendency for cooperation."

She questioned why the human female lives far beyond her childbearing age and goes through the menopause, which other primates do not. Since the human female evolved into the only primate who is able to live many years beyond her child bearing years she was able to care for the children her daughters were bearing and give them individual attention as they grew and developed new skills and emotional attachments.

We humans are not able to care for ourselves as early as

other primates so we need someone to take care of us as we grow and learn. In caring for her grandchild the grandmother learned new things which she was able to teach because she had the time and realized the importance of what she had learned. Men were too busy with manly things and younger women were too busy with baby things so here comes grandma. Now a child has someone who not only can take care of her physical needs, but can also help her notice a flower or a butterfly. If she gets hurt there is someone who cares and has the time to help.

Hawkes also states that without menopause " all children would still be dependent on their mothers for survival, so once older mothers died, many young offspring would die too. Grandmothering gave us the kind of upbringing that made us more dependent on each other socially and prone to engage each others attention. This trend, drove the increase in brain size, along with longer lifespan."

So, you see, even before history was being recorded, Old Ladies were shaping and helping us develop as humans. We certainly cannot let our jobs become obsolete now when there is so much which needs to be remembered and done and who is better than us, Old Ladies, to do them? We, who have experienced all phases of life, know what is important to pass on to our children and what is best to let go of. We don't have the strength and energy to carry heavy loads of used up useless things which seemed so important when we were younger, so what we pass on will be what creates the kind of people who love each other and love all things living and not living in our universe, things of the mind and spirit and the God which is Love.

Credits

William Sloan Colfin, author of "Credo" page 51

Robert Becker M. D. "The Body Erlectric" page 53

Condace Pert Ph. D. "Molecules of Emotion" page 57

Elisabeth Kubler-Ross M.D. "On Death and Dying" page 69

Wendy McCord Ph. D. "Earth Babies" page 204

The World Needs Old Ladies

Gladys Taylor McGarey, M.D., M.D. (H), has been a family physician for more than sixty years. She is board certified in Holistic and Integrated Medicine. She is internationally known for her pioneering work in holistic medicine, natural birthing and the physician-patient partnership. She was the co-founder of the American Holistic Medical Foundation. She is known as the Mother of Holistic Medicine. Her work through her foundation, The Foundation For Living Medicine has helped expand the knowledge and application of holistic principles through scientific research and education. She and her Foundation are currently actively involved in healthcare reform. Their recently published position papers that articulate a new vision for healthcare are widely distributed. She is author of three books, "The Physician Within You," "Born To Live," and "Living Medicine."

Pioneering Accomplishments Include:
- Co-Founder, the American Holistic Medical Association
- Pioneered Fathers in the Delivery Room
- Co-Founder, the Academy of Parapsychology and Medicine
- Created only ARE Clinic based on the work of Edgar Cayce
- First to utilize acupuncture in the US and trained other physicians how to use it
- The International Academy of Clinical Hypnosis began in her living room

- Founded the Gladys Taylor McGarey Medical Foundation to bridge the gap between holistic and traditional medicine.
- Taught safer birthing practices to rural women in Afghanistan resulting in a 47% decrease in infant and small child mortality
- Created a task force comprised of more than 100 holistic physicians and other professional healthcare providers to envision a new medical model in response to the need for healthcare reform and work toward its implementation

---

Bare words and stories Eveline Horelle Dailey use to capture her nature and to explore her personal potential makes her a writer.

She paints when a canvas calls for it; she weaves when the rhythm of the loom demands attention but she writes and dances with her muse.

French brings texture to her prose.

Not afraid to cross the literary bridge at the center of her mind she writes with passion for those with similar intellect. Her inspirations come from nature and people; they are the source of the colors she sees, and they give birth to the distinct complexion of her writing style.

She is read internationally and continues her endeavors as a public speaker, writer, philanthropist, painter and weaver. She is a multiple awards recipient and member of various associations of writers.

Gladys T. McGarey

The World Needs Old Ladies